Serving At-Risk Teens

Proven Strategies and Programs for Bridging the Gap

ANGELA CRAIG

CHANTELL L. MCDOWELL

Neal-Schuman
An imprint of the American Library Association
Chicago   2013

Printed in the United States of America

17 16 15 14 13   5 4 3 2 1

Extensive effort has gone into ensuring the reliability of the information in this book; however, the publisher makes no warranty, express or implied, with respect to the material contained herein.

ISBNs: 978-1-55570-760-6 (paper); 978-1-55570-948-8 (PDF).

Library of Congress Cataloging-in-Publication Data
Craig, Angela.
  Serving at-risk teens : proven strategies and programs for bridging the gap / Angela Craig, Chantell L. McDowell.
    pages cm
  Includes bibliographical references and index.
  ISBN 978-1-55570-760-6
  1. Young adults' libraries—United States. 2. Libraries and teenagers—United States. 3. Libraries and juvenile delinquents—United States. I. McDowell, Chantell L. II. Title.

Z718.5.C73 2013
027.62'60973—dc23

2012044857

Book design in Bembo and Optima by UB Communications.
Cover design by Rosemary Holderby/Cole Design and Production.

⊚ This paper meets the requirements of ANSI/NISO Z39.48-1992 (Permanence of Paper).

Contents

Preface

Serving At-Risk Teens: Proven Strategies and Programs for Bridging the Gap details the best practices, pertinent suggestions, and personal experiences of librarians and staff members nationwide who work with at-risk teens. This book's publication coincides with an immense economic crisis in American society that has adversely impacted funding for libraries and their services. Even in the best economic times library services for teens, whether at risk or not, tend to be underfunded, understaffed, or overlooked. As libraries of all types are caught in an economic downturn, cuts to teen services come at a time when the at-risk population is growing at an exponential rate.

The phrase "at risk" typically has negative connotations, and the average person's perception of what an at-risk teen looks and acts like is not a flattering picture. With the best of intentions, society often tries to place teens who meet certain criteria, whether based upon socioeconomic, racial, and/or familial backgrounds, into at-risk programs with the goal of helping those teens. However, the label "at risk" can follow these young people into their adult lives and have a detrimental effect upon how they perceive themselves and how the world perceives and reacts to them.

With a growing number of at-risk adolescents in both urban and rural areas of the country, libraries and communities need to work together to find new ways to serve this population. These teens can be the most rewarding patrons with whom a librarian works, while simultaneously being the most challenging. This book does not intend to glamorize a certain demographic of adolescents or excuse destructive or harmful teen behavior. Some of the teens interviewed and profiled for this book have committed crimes that have sent them to detention facilities, alternative schools, or youth offender programs; others are average teenagers who can be found in any neighborhood or school.

Chapter 1 focuses on making a case for library services for at-risk teens even when many organizations are understaffed with limited budgets. Chapter 2 focuses on understanding the needs of at-risk teens as well as their own expectations of library programs. Chapter 3 addresses the diversity of the at-risk population and how libraries can provide services for these many-faceted youth. Chapter 4 defines the types of facilities in which at-risk youth may be housed and how libraries can navigate these facilities' systems in order to provide services to teens. Chapter 5 details the role of library staff members when working with at-risk teens and also helps determine if offering services for this group is a good fit for their staff and library. Chapter 6 explores the literacy and reading needs of at-risk teens and methods for developing a diverse and appealing collection. Chapter 7 explores technology and how it can interest this population in a constructive manner. Chapter 8 details the library systems currently providing innovative services to at-risk teens, both within their own libraries and with partner organizations. Chapter 9 furnishes techniques to evaluate the library programs for at-risk teens and explains how to obtain measurable results. The book ends with three additional resources: Appendix A offers examples of forms used with the programs and best practices detailed in Chapter 8 and throughout the text; Appendix B provides a list of organizations that serve at-risk teens—organizations that teens can join and organizations that make public policy regarding youth at risk; and an annotated bibliography lists books recommended for library staff to engage the youth at risk.

Libraries across the country have used every program presented in this book to engage and educate at-risk teens about the benefits of library services. Although the programs have a proven record of success with at-risk teens, our purpose in writing this book is not to encourage libraries to create carbon copies of past programs, but to utilize this information as a starting point for developing their own programs that will work for their teen patrons and their circumstances, whatever they may be. This book's methodologies are designed to challenge librarians and library staff members who work with adolescents to see teens' potential, and not just their label.

Acknowledgments

This book would not have been possible without the encouragement and support of my editor, Michele Gorman, whom I count as a friend and colleague. Thank you, Chantell McDowell, my coauthor and partner, whose experience and perspective gave this book a depth I could not have achieved alone. Chapter 7 could never have happened without Kelly Czarnecki, another friend and colleague, who is an amazing resource for technology services to teens and is the most devoted person I know to serving at-risk youth. Thank you also to Margo Fesperman, librarian extraordinaire with the Mecklenburg County Sheriff's Department. You do every day what needs to be done with youthful offenders, and you inspire others in the process. This book features the innovations and insights of some of the most talented library staff and community partners I have encountered. I am so grateful for your contributions to this book and humbled by your commitment to at-risk teens. Thank you for sharing your expertise! Thank you to my library system, the Charlotte Mecklenburg Library, for providing me with such wonderful opportunities for growth and challenging me to work with at-risk teens, which quickly became my favorite population. Thank you to my mother, Sue Copass, my beta reader who edited this book one chapter at a time. Thank you to my husband, Donovan Craig, for your constant support and understanding while I worked on "my project." I could not have done it without you.

I dedicate this book to library staff who serve at-risk youth, wherever they may be. I hope you find this book helpful; I hope it validates your hard work; and I hope that it inspires fellow library staff members to follow in your footsteps and work with at-risk teens. Most of all I dedicate this book to the teens, everywhere, who are thirsty for knowledge and new experiences. I hope you know that you will always have a place at the library.

—Angela Craig

This is my first venture in writing a book. It has been an interesting experience to research and write a book on a topic that I feel so passionate about, serving at-risk teens. First, I would like to extend my deepest appreciation to Angela Craig for giving me the wonderful opportunity to write and the confidence in me to deliver. She has been a great motivator. Angela and I share an understanding of at-risk teens and have become friends while writing this book together. It was an interesting journey, and I sincerely appreciate her patience and ongoing encouragement while writing, reviewing, and editing this book. I must also thank our editor, Michele Gorman, who forged the connection between Angela and me. Without her active persuasion and encouragement, I would not be the coauthor of this book.

As a first-time writer, I honestly didn't know my writing abilities, but my family and friends were very supportive and I appreciate them for that. Thank you to Brooklyn Public Library for giving me the opportunity to work at the New Lots branch and providing me with sufficient library resources to make a difference in the lives of my at-risk Brooklyn teens. Thank you to Charlotte Mecklenburg Library, for taking me on board and sincerely believing in me. Thank you for your extraordinary commitment to bringing out the best in me. Your dedication to my career development has touched me and greatly inspired me to continue working diligently toward serving all teens.

Thank you to my mother, Theresa McDowell, who pushed me to no end, encouraged me to take first steps, taught me how to make the right choices in the direction of change, and patiently guided me through the unwritten lessons of life.

Thanks go to the love of my life, Donald Edge III, for your constant support and understanding while I spent the last few months searching for my destiny. Thank you for always being there for me, and never doubting my dreams, no matter how crazy they might be. You are my inspiration in everything I do and every choice I make. I could not have done any of this without you. You still make my heart sing joyous melodies.

Michelle T. McDowell George, my big sister, thank you for being a true inspiration throughout my entire growing process and encouraging me every step of the way. Makia McDowell, although you are my niece, you have motivated me to reach for something better than what was expected of me and you continue to be an inspiration to me; I thank you for being my best friend. Thank you to my niece, Jasmine R. George, and goddaughter, Isis

McLemore, for giving me a reason to work hard; I know you both are following my lead and I want to make you proud.

I also owe a debt of gratitude to many other librarians and library staff who have touched my life and believed in me over the years, starting with Tierra Blanchard, Evelena, Bethina, Liz, Sam, Greg B., Shabazz (New Lots 2008), Nikeya Jarrett, Joycelyn Maynard, Shirley H., Yvette Jenkins, Vinette Thomas, Sandra Sajonas, Nate Hill, and Nick Higgins. Thanks also go to the Pratt Institute Registrar's Staff, Domonick, Sabrina, Toya, Charlotte, Cynthia, and Matt, whom I have considered mentors and friends ever since I began my journey in librarianship.

—Chantell L. McDowell

INTRODUCTION

Looking Beyond the Labels

Historically, troubled adolescents have been called many names. From the clinical term "juvenile delinquents" to the more insensitive "hoodlums" or "thugs," there is a certain group of young people who fall into the category of "problematic." The current label for these adolescents is "at risk," yet what does this term really tell us? When we picture at-risk teenagers and we are honest with ourselves, typically the image is not very flattering. We might think of at-risk teens as troublemakers, or more trouble than they're worth. Normally an at-risk teen is not a youth who is "library ready" or even a traditional library user. However, it has been proven time and again that patrons who are nontraditional library users, such as at-risk youth, are the patrons who need the library the most.

The foundation of this text started as a simple question: How can libraries better serve at-risk teens? The concept seemed straightforward, yet when researching material for this book we realized that libraries first have to define what, exactly, an at-risk teen is. At-risk teens have been defined as "adolescents whose potential of becoming healthy and productive adults is reduced because they are at high risk of encountering serious problems at home, in school, or in their communities" (Trachtman, 1991: 28). In the context of the library world, we will define an at-risk teen as an adolescent, aged twelve through eighteen, whose developmental, intellectual, emotional, educational, and information needs are not being met, which potentially places them behind their peers and hinders their successful transition into adulthood.

As a librarian with the Charlotte Mecklenburg Library system, Angela works with the whole spectrum of at-risk teens, from high school students to youthful offenders, teen parents, alternative school students, and beyond. She has had wonderful experiences with each of them, many of which were the inspiration for this book. None of the youth in her programs ever labeled themselves or their fellow teens as "at risk," although they were familiar with the term. During one of Angela's first programs, the group discussed labels and what they mean. She asked the participants, who were aged fifteen through seventeen, what they thought the label "at-risk teen" meant. The teens responded:

"Those are the bad kids."
"The ones that are always causing trouble."
"The ones that the teachers don't like."
"The kids that are in those special programs that never work."
"Those are the thug kids."
"The kids that aren't going anywhere."

The class took place at an alternative high school as part of a library outreach program, and the students themselves were what many would denote as "at risk." However, these kids were the furthest from the at-risk stereotype as one could get. They were motivated readers—interested in books and discussing them—and were some of Angela's best patrons. They weren't "those teens," they were just teens. It was a pivotal experience which demonstrated that teens are always more than the label they are given.

During another library program that was in partnership with a juvenile detention center, Angela facilitated a four-week technology class for male youthful offenders, aged sixteen through seventeen. The program went very well and the youth worked hard to complete their video project, which was a commercial for the detention center library. Right before the last class, Angela created certificates of achievement for the participants. She passed them out at the end of the session and gave each boy a round of applause. One of the boys stared at his certificate, and Angela became concerned that she had misspelled his name. When she asked if there was something wrong with his certificate, the boy replied, "No, I've just never gotten a certificate before. I'm gonna hang this up on my wall so I can look at it, both here and when I get home." If a certificate created on a whim could be so inspiring to a youth at risk, imagine the effect a focused effort would have on these patrons.

Chantell McDowell began her career at the Brooklyn Public Library, New Lots branch, located in the East New York section of Brooklyn. As the young adult librarian she was instantly surrounded by teens who were all considered at risk. The New Lots branch had been her neighborhood library growing up and just like her teen patrons, she too had been considered at risk throughout her childhood. In her role, Chantell worked to make a difference with her patrons, particularly with the youth at risk. She immediately began creating programs and providing services that she knew would benefit her teen patrons.

One of the first programs Chantell created was a rap session program, which allowed the teens to gather and talk about anything. This was very successful because it gave teens an opportunity to voice their opinions and connect with other teens. She discovered that many of the teens who visited the library and participated in the program had additional, almost adult, responsibilities in their lives. Some teens had been abandoned by their parents. Some teens attended alternative high schools, while others struggled in regular high school. Some teens were confused and lonely and were looking for a safe place to hang out. Teens came to her branch to ask questions about their homework, to complain about their teachers, to get help researching a topic, or to participate in the programs that offered snacks because they were hungry. There were teens who didn't go to school because they didn't have transportation or appropriate clothes, or they had to watch their younger siblings. Some teens who had dropped out of school came to the library to hang out with their friends and hear about what was happening at their former school. Many pretended they were taking classes to get their GED, not letting their friends know just how difficult life had become. All the teens in Chantell's programs depended on library services to satisfy their needs in some capacity. During one of the rap sessions, a few teens opened up about their experiences. Even now, Chantell can recall what they talked about:

> "I have a lot of issues at home. I hate going to school because it is hard and I don't understand. I don't have a father; my mother is always working so I come to the library just to chill with you and my friends. It's lonely at home."
>
> Another said, "I am tired of babysitting my brothers and sisters. I never get a chance to be a kid. I am so tired of people telling me what they think I should do."

One seventeen-year-old girl, who was in her last year of high school, said she was pregnant and couldn't tell her mother. She explained that her mother had a baby two months ago and she was scared to tell her about her pregnancy. She asked Chantell for advice, but Chantell was stuck. "I'm a librarian," Chantell thought, "not a certified counselor." What could she do? This was one of the many encounters with at-risk teens that required Chantell to step outside of her role as a traditional librarian and connect a patron with a professional who was more qualified to help. It was something that Chantell encountered many times while serving her teen population, and she quickly became familiar with the proper channels to guide them to if they needed assistance outside of her capabilities.

At-risk teens (whether they admit it or not) need a mentor, a motivator, a friend, and a confidant. In many ways, a youth librarian is a staff member who can fill that role. As information professionals, we operate outside of the normal parameters of school, parents, and teachers. We can offer teens access to information, books, and ideas that can stretch and challenge their perspective of the world. We cannot, and should not, try to take the place of other youth-serving professionals, such as counselors and social workers. However, we can let teens use the library as their refuge. We can talk with teens about pop culture and have fun facilitating teen programs. And we can, if need be, connect at-risk patrons to resources and organizations that guide them through a difficult situation, when the library cannot.

The authors' experiences working with at-risk teens, along with an obvious publishing gap on the subject of library services for youth at risk, presented a need for this text. There are a handful of resources, some current, many out-of-date, that pertain to this subject. While at-risk youth are highlighted in library texts and articles, there is not a current book that focuses solely on the population. This text seeks to provide hands-on accounts from libraries that have developed best practices for serving the at-risk population. Most important, this book is designed to look at the at-risk population from a library perspective so that any institution—whether public, private, academic, or school media—can create initiatives that will meet the needs of these adolescents.

Society tends to generalize that the at-risk teen population comes from low-income or underprivileged backgrounds. Research has shown that teenagers who are high risk often live in disadvantaged settings (Druian and Butler,

1987). Circumstances linked with being at risk include coming from a poor family with an ethnic and linguistic minority background, having parents who are not high school graduates, and having a negative self-perception. Other factors that contribute to teenage at-risk behaviors are:

- living in high-growth states,
- living in unstable school districts,
- having low academic skills (though not necessarily low intelligence), and
- being the children of single parents (Druian and Butler, 1987).

While these are valid conditions and do represent divisions of the at-risk population, it is imperative for libraries, schools, and youth facilities to acknowledge that socioeconomic standing and ethnic backgrounds are not the only factors that can place teens in jeopardy. Teens who come from a stable home environment and have supportive adults in their lives can just as easily be at risk for drug or alcohol addiction, teenage pregnancy, dropping out of school, suicide, gang activity, bullying, depression, or not reaching their full potential. "At risk" is a label, and labels for teens can be a tricky thing. Youth are labeled more or less the second they enter any environment, whether it be academic, sports-related, social, or any other realm where adolescents are found. However, the authors have yet to find a teen who identifies himself or herself as at risk unless an adult has already done so. And once a youth is identified as at risk, many of the adults who work with and interact with the youth end up serving the label and not the actual teen.

Admittedly one could argue that all teens are at risk in one way or another, but that is not entirely true. The term denotes a certain demographic of teen, yet it is a demographic that is quickly growing and the definition of what it means to be "at risk" is expanding. "Disconnected youth" is a term now used in relation to teens at risk. This rising population consists of youth who are not enrolled in school or do not have a form of employment. For various reasons they are disengaged from society and are more likely to engage in crime, become incarcerated, become homeless, and/or rely on public systems of support (U.S. Government Accountability Office, 2008). The youth of today face different challenges than those of even ten years ago. The pace of society is faster with information spreading quickly, requiring teens to keep up or they will be left behind. When speaking with counselors, social workers, and behavioral therapists who work with the at-risk population, the authors were told again and again that it is much easier to fall through the cracks in the system as schools, juvenile facilities, and public services scramble to keep up with the demands of an ever-increasing at-risk teenage population.

How can libraries serve the needs of the youth at risk? By their nature, libraries are already set up to be wonderful resources for the teen population. Libraries provide free access to materials, computers, programs, and resources that help to educate teens and keep them connected to the world around them. Now, libraries have to take the initiative and make service to the at-risk population a priority. Many libraries across the nation are doing just that, with great success. Most if not all of the programs and library initiatives featured in this text were tailored for a specific teen population. The at-risk population is not a group where one program type fits all. There are many levels of needs within this demographic, and the need that the library can most successfully meet is informational. Libraries can help at-risk teens keep pace with their peers and compete in a world that is increasingly dependent on technology and those who are proficient in its use. By working to serve all teens, libraries can bridge the gap between those who have access to information resources and those who do not.

References

Druian, Greg, and Jocelyn A. Butler. 1987. "Effective Schooling Practices and At-Risk Youth: What the Research Shows." *School Improvement Research Series*, Topical Synthesis #1. Portland, OR: Northwest Educational Research Laboratory. http://educationnorthwest.org/webfm_send/520.

Trachtman, Roberta. 1991. "Early Childhood Education and Child Care: Issues of At-Risk Children and Families." *Urban Education* 26: 28.

U.S. Government Accountability Office. 2008. *Disconnected Youth: Federal Action Could Address Some of the Challenges Faced by Local Programs That Reconnect Youth to Education and Employment*. Report to the Chairman, Committee on Education and Labor, House of Representatives. Washington, DC: U.S Government Accountability Office. http://www.gao.gov/new.items/d08313.pdf.

CHAPTER 1

Services for At-Risk Teens

The American Library Association's annual *State of America's Libraries* report for 2010 affirms that the beginning of the new decade is "a perfect storm of growing demand and shrinking resources" (ALA, 2010: 1). In the aftermath of the 2007–2009 recession, which some financial experts have compared to the Great Depression, libraries throughout the country have become many people's only source for information, access to computers, entertainment, continuing education, and employment resources. However, the recession has proven to be a double-edged sword for libraries. Although the lagging economy has driven people of all ages to their libraries in record numbers, funding for libraries has also lagged. Many libraries, whether they are public, academic, private, or school media, have been forced to cut programs, cut operating hours, lay off staff members, or even close their facilities. School media centers nationwide have faced severe budget cuts and layoffs, or in many cases, are no longer given control over their designated funds (Allen and Bradley, 2009). Due to drastic budget cuts and staff shortages, the momentum that the teen services movement gained in libraries during the first decade of the twenty-first century seems to be at a standstill. With shrinking library budgets and reduction in staff and operating hours, library services for teen patrons, and by extension teens at risk, have declined or stalled as libraries scramble to keep their doors open and to make ends meet.

Beginning even before the latest recession, young adults have been routinely underrepresented in terms of library budget, programming, collection development, specialized staff, and outreach. The at-risk population garners even less attention since they are typically lower performing in sports and academics, two areas where high-performing teens can find almost unlimited support. Library services for at-risk teens are crucial because they are often the ones to be neglected when libraries reduce budgets and programs, ultimately placing them even further behind their peers. Despite these challenges, this book's fundamental position is that libraries and their staff, working in partnerships within their communities, can make a considerable, positive impact on the lives of young adults by striving to meet their informational needs. Working with at-risk teenagers can be one of the most rewarding experiences for library staff and also one of the most challenging. At-risk teens are often non-traditional library users who may or may not see the value of having a library card and using it. However, it is worth the effort for libraries to reach out to at-risk teens because this population benefits greatly from library services, and in turn the library itself benefits from working with at-risk teens.

According to a study completed by the Wallace Foundation, library-based youth development programs can provide both specific job skills and personal and social development for teens (Spielberger, Horton, and Michels, 2004). Additionally, these programs can provide opportunities for teens to develop positive relationships with adults and peers and increase their knowledge, appreciation, and use of the library. From a library standpoint, youth programs can improve the skills and attitudes of library staff working with teens, fostering more positive attitudes toward youth among library staff. Changing the mind-set of staff regarding teens can influence the "broader culture of the library and lead to future positive interactions" (Spielberger, Horton, and Michels, 2004: 6). The study indicated that "more positive staff attitudes towards teens generally have a positive impact on a library's ability to attract youth patrons and interact with them in developmentally appropriate ways" (Spielberger, Horton, and Michels, 2004: 6). As staff continues to be educated about the needs of at-risk teens and how the library can provide appropriate services, libraries become a more welcoming environment and a preferred destination for teens.

Why Serve At-Risk Teens?

The question of why libraries should provide services to youth at risk is asked by policy makers, library staff, library patrons, community organizations, and sometimes from the teens themselves. What role does a library have in the lives of youth at risk? The answer is that libraries provide valuable and potentially life-changing resources to which at-risk youth might otherwise not have access. Libraries can best serve youth at risk by providing the services they excel at: offering access to technology, supplying educational support, developing interest in books and reading, and helping meet the informational needs of their adolescent patrons.

Margaret Edwards, author of the classic young adult librarianship book *The Fair Garden and the Swarm of Beasts: The Library and the Young Adult*, wrote that "there is no age group more important than the young adults, who in a few short years will be guiding the destiny of this nation" (Edwards, 1994: 14). Teens, at risk or otherwise, will quickly grow into adults, who will ultimately become the community leaders and decision makers regarding library funding and development. It is a reasonable assumption that if teens are made to feel welcome in libraries, have staff and collections dedicated to their needs, and are taught the value of libraries, they will support library initiatives as adults. It is also reasonable to assume that if libraries are not welcoming toward adolescents, as adults they will not support library development. Libraries have traditionally devoted the majority of their resources to services for children and adults, with teen services either added on to one of the departments or ignored. With the adolescent population growing at an exponential rate, this practice needs to change. Teen services should not be an afterthought or attached to another department; to make an impact with young adults, libraries need to dedicate staff, budget, and resources exclusively to the teen population. With focused efforts aimed at teens, libraries are building their future patron base. As libraries develop resources for teen patrons, they must also make a place for at-risk teens.

The library is in a unique position to help all teens, especially those at risk, meet the increasingly demanding information needs of today's society. Public libraries and school media centers have always been hubs for teen information needs. Libraries support teens by providing readers' advisory services, creating booklists, assisting with homework, supplying resources regarding colleges and careers, and providing access to technology. These resources are especially important for at-risk teens, who may or may not have an adult in their life providing guidance about higher education, vocational training, and career opportunities. Libraries can also play an instrumental role in the lives of at-risk teens by offering diverse programs and services that provide opportunities to realize their creative and developmental potential. Offering programs based on areas of high teen interest allows at-risk youth to tap into their own experiences and express themselves in ways that are personal, positive, and empowering.

In providing services to youth at risk, libraries have the opportunity to make a significant and measurable impact with a high-need patron base within their community. While this serves the greater good of any given community, it also establishes a place of importance for libraries and continually demonstrates the institution's relevance in twenty-first-century culture. If libraries do not indicate that they value all teens, including at-risk teens—which in turn leads young adults to value their libraries—then libraries themselves are at risk of becoming obsolete.

Advocating for Outreach Services

Interviews with librarians, library staff, counselors, teachers, community partners, and administrators resulted in the overwhelming response that the best way to engage at-risk teenagers is through outreach initiatives. Supervising Librarian–Teen Services Coordinator Pham Condello of the Ocean County Library System (Ocean County, NJ) states that outreach is one of the key components when establishing a presence with at-risk teens and in acquiring teen participation within library branches. "You need to go to them, including those who are incarcerated, in school, or living in group homes. Meeting with these outside organizations and creating ongoing relationships is a valuable tool," said Condello (Pham Condello, e-mail/phone interview, February 22, 2012).

Outreach services provide access to library resources that the at-risk population may not otherwise have contact with. At-risk teens may face obstacles that prevent them from utilizing the library, such as lack of transportation. Other barriers can be social, such as a lack of awareness of library resources or not prioritizing educational pursuits. Emotional obstacles, such as feeling unwelcome in a library setting, can also deter teens from utilizing the library. Outreach services to teens can help overcome these barriers and make the library an approachable entity and one they seek out after becoming aware of its presence. By reaching out to these young people libraries will "stimulate the discovery of knowledge, provide resources that can improve the quality of life for all community residents, and promote intellectual freedom and lifelong learning" (Meadows, 2004: 2).

Although there are tremendous benefits to outreach, providing these services can be challenging for libraries in the best of budgetary times and seemingly impossible in the worst. For as many reasons as one can find to facilitate outreach to youth at risk, one can also cite many counterarguments. For example:

- Lack of funding, resources, appropriate training, and staff time can easily prohibit libraries from even attempting to plan an outreach initiative.
- Library staff may not be aware of the needs of youth at risk or how to serve them.
- Partnerships with youth-serving facilities may be difficult for libraries to maintain as resources are dispersed to other departments or taken away all together.
- Library administration may not support outreach initiatives to any population, much less to at-risk teens. It is also not uncommon for decision makers to feel that at-risk teens do not deserve outreach initiatives to begin with, because they might see this population as "bad" or even dangerous, and they might view other patron groups as more "worthy" of library resources.

These concerns and counterarguments are valid and should be addressed by library staff if they are seeking to provide outreach to youth at risk. To make a case for outreach services, libraries must demonstrate the need and how the programs benefit the library. The following are suggestions for how to make a case for outreach programs to at-risk teens:

- Put a face to the teen who will benefit from the services. It is easy for decision makers to turn away services to a faceless patron, yet more difficult when the patron in need is identified as a teen mother looking for a storytime for her child, a youthful offender wanting to participate in a book club, or a teen who needs help applying for college. Youth at risk is a population that needs to be defined outside of its labels. Too often when decision makers hear the term "at risk" it conjures negative connotations. "At risk" is a term that should be used sparingly when identifying this population. Instead, libraries must identify the needs of the teens and draw the focus to how the library can assist.
- Outreach programs to at-risk teens can provide libraries with a unique opportunity to collaborate with organizations, groups, and leaders that can enhance the library's standing in the community. Libraries need a positive and visible presence in their community and outreach services are an excellent way to demonstrate what the library mission is and how it benefits society at large. Collaborating with organizations that

serve at-risk teens gives the library a presence within the community and a potential ally when advocating for services for at-risk teens. Outreach programs also give libraries a method to measure their impact within their community, and illustrate why library services are needed.

- Outreach helps the library keep in touch with current issues and needs within the at-risk community, and can help shape library programming into more effective services. At times, libraries can become too insular and fall out of touch with what is happening within their community. By venturing into the populace, the library is keeping tabs on what is most needed by its patrons. The benefits are twofold because this helps with outreach initiatives as well as services provided within the library.

- Having even a small outreach initiative aimed at youth at risk is significantly better than having no initiative at all. By their own directives, libraries must provide equal access to services for every patron, and outreach to underserved populations achieves that aim. Even with limited staff and budgets, libraries have different outreach options. Deposit collections, volunteer-lead programs, or strategic visits to youth facilities and schools can make a huge impact within the teen population. Exposure and access to library services are critical when connecting with at-risk youth. Outreach initiatives make the library visible and approachable to teens, which can put them on the path to becoming library users.

If outreach to the at-risk population is still not possible, it is recommended that staff be patient and broach the subject again when there is more flexibility with library resources. While outreach is on hold, library staff can continue to make connections within the at-risk population. Broker relationships with organizations that serve youth at risk and keep tabs on the needs of the population. Draft proposals for initiatives and have items ready for submission for the next fiscal year. Even if libraries are not currently facilitating outreach initiatives, they can stay aware of the needs of the population and work on future programs that can be put in place when the time is right for outreach.

Strategies for Gaining Support for At-Risk Initiatives

In order for any initiative to succeed it must have the combined support of staff, library administration, and library policy makers. The success of a program also depends upon the commitment of personnel who are invested in the well-being of the library, such as the library director, library board, Friends of the Library committees, public and private school principals, Parent-Teacher Organizations, and youth-serving organizations, as well as the staff facilitating the initiatives. The support of these entities and individuals can secure a place for at-risk teens within libraries as well as the inclusion of their needs in library policy. When advocating for teen-focused services, libraries should make certain that donating organizations, individual supporters, and policy makers are aware of the needs of the at-risk population and that they are included in future decisions regarding library funding and policies.

An unfortunate truth is that in times of budget reductions, services that are not part of library policy are often the first cut and, once cut, difficult to reinstate. Assessment of the at-risk population and how it fits into library policy is essential when soliciting support for current or future programs. To assess the at-risk population and how the library can best offer service, staff can take these initial steps:

- Research the number of young adults in the community or schools and determine if factors are present that put some of the population at risk. If so, how can the library respond?
- Complete a thorough inventory of the library's collection, programs, and resources that are offered to teens. Do they contain diversity and have broad appeal? Do library materials appeal to enthusiastic teen patrons, reluctant readers, and nontraditional library users? Are materials current, or are they outdated? How can the library resolve any gaps in service or materials?
- Are there barriers in the library preventing teens from utilizing the services? Would a teen, at risk or otherwise, want to come to the library?
- Survey the young people the library wants to serve and specifically seek out teen groups underrepresented at the library. Determine what is preventing them from utilizing the library, how their needs are not being met, and how the library can assist them.
- Has the library staff undergone training that is focused on young adult development? Is the library staff aware of current teen trends in literature, pop culture, music, movies, etc? Can the staff connect with the teens?
- What are the projected outcomes of teen programming, and how do they benefit the patrons and library as a whole?

After completing the assessment, prepare a brief report signifying how the library can best attend to the needs of at-risk teens, and detail how this fits into the library mission. Keep expectations manageable, especially if this is the first time the library has ever considered implementing programs and policies specifically tailored to at-risk teens.

Libraries that have never included a place for at-risk teens in their policies will want to have a goal in mind when endorsing services for this population. Clearly define the population the library intends to work with and outline how the organization will serve it. A plan with targeted efforts will garner support more easily than an unorganized effort that does not have clear guidelines or specifically address the patrons' needs. Even if libraries already facilitate some services for at-risk teens, a more focused effort to organize library policy in their favor is most effective.

Do not become discouraged if a new program or policy is not implemented the first time it is presented. Remember to enlist support from other agencies in the community. Ask about their best practices and if they are willing to share any data that could further an at-risk program. Do not forget to look at other libraries in similar communities and schools with active young adult programs and analyze their best practices and success stories, such as the ones found in this book. Serving at-risk teens takes dedication, a firm belief in the program, patience, and often, tenacity.

Involving Library Staff: Utilizing Talent and Enlisting Reluctant Employees

Perhaps one of the greatest challenges when serving at-risk teenagers is finding library employees who are a good fit for this population. Suggestions for desirable staff skills include the following:

- Enthusiasm
- Ability to connect with teens
- Patience
- Interest in young adult literature
- Positive attitude
- Empathy toward teens
- Flexibility
- Sense of humor

- Knowledge of basic adolescent development principles
- Ability to collaborate with teens and adults
- Creative programming ideas
- Comfortable with teens from a variety of backgrounds, and with different abilities
- Genuine interest in working with young adults

A common mistake many librarians make when serving this population is to assume they need to be experts on all matters regarding teens, which can overwhelm them to the point that they do not attempt to facilitate any teen programs, much less an at-risk teen program. In contrast, another mistake that some librarians make is to assume that they *are* experts about teenagers, when in fact they might be out of touch with current issues or not be the strongest person to lead a particular teen program. When their experience is limited, library staff might consider having a qualified guest speaker lead discussions on teen topics. Young adults, especially those at risk, are a sensitive population and can sense when adults are feigning interest or do not want to interact with them. When trying to engage adolescents who are typically nonlibrary users, librarians will want to do everything possible to make certain their library experiences are positive.

It is advisable to choose carefully the staff members who work with adolescents, especially at-risk teens. Staff buy-in is essential to the success of any library program or service that focuses on at-risk teens. Although librarians need the support of library administrators to get new initiatives off the ground, they must also have the support of the staff members who will be implementing the programs and interacting with teen patrons. Working with at-risk teens is not every staff person's career goal, and staff may encounter colleagues who are not supportive or do not see any value in serving this population. To combat this, one can create a list of every department that will come in contact, either directly or indirectly, with the at-risk teens and supply those offices with information about the programs. Youth librarians and staff are advised to educate their colleagues about the at-risk population and explain why the library is working to serve the teens. Often libraries can help smooth the way for teen programs and partnerships by taking the time to work with staff members who typically do not serve teens.

In a public library setting, communication outreach can include departments such as the circulation staff, security, adult services, maintenance, reference, technology services, managers, and children's services. School media centers will want to inform teachers, educational departments, office staff, technology support, maintenance, and administrators. In both environments, these staff can ultimately give strong advocacy for at-risk teen programs, especially if they are invested in the initiative. Librarians can communicate directly with staff members about the programs being implemented by sending e-mails to employees, contacting them by phone, or talking to them individually, all of which provide the courtesy of informing them about new teen programs or services.

In addition to the departments within their library, staff can also inform organizations that support the system, such as the Friends of the Library or the Parent-Teacher Organization. Make all communications positive and inclusive. Although not all staff and departments will be working directly with the at-risk teens, their support will help further future initiatives. Libraries might find more teen services advocates among the staff, or they might find resistance. Policies and approval from library administration to which librarians can refer are beneficial in case they come across colleagues who are not accommodating regarding new initiatives. As always, education is the best way to combat resistance. Just as librarians let library administrators know about the needs of at-risk youth and how they can benefit from the library, they should also inform library staff at all levels. The employees as well as policy makers who directly interact with at-risk teens need to be familiar with and sensitive to the needs of these adolescents. This will make facilitating programs and providing services for this unique teen group easier and their library experience more enjoyable.

To further support library employees who interact with at-risk teens, librarians must become familiar with various social work applications and standards regarding at-risk youth. This does *not* at all imply that librarians should take on the responsibility of a social worker. However, becoming knowledgeable about basic directives can help when libraries create their own policies in support of at-risk teens. Enlisting the help of a professional, such as a social worker or guidance counselor, can assist library staff as they create policies regarding at-risk teens and help better serve the population.

As librarians create directives to include the at-risk population, they will want to create policies to ensure their own safety and the safety of library patrons. Having these policies in place does not mean that the library regards at-risk youth as a "bad" or "dangerous" population. On the contrary, clearly detailed policies provide library staff with resources to utilize when working with a population whose needs differ from those of other patrons. If properly implemented, these policies will help not only staff members, but also the patrons for whom they are designed. For example, does the library have a policy in place that specifies how to assist homeless teens? Does the library have a policy that specifies how to handle teenage gang activity? What about policies on cyberbullying? Too often teens are lumped in with the children's department policies and guidelines, or they are overlooked altogether. Libraries must know how to support all teens and what resources the staff can utilize. The more information and tools provided to the library staff, the more confident they will feel when interacting with at-risk teens.

Strength in Numbers and Community Partners: Libraries Are Not Alone

To effectively advocate for at-risk teens, it is beneficial for librarians to collaborate by forming productive partnerships with other community organizations that serve this population. Strength resides in numbers and when serving at-risk youth, libraries can be a powerful ally and provide much-needed resources to community groups who work with teens.

Building a strong relationship with community organizations takes time. When working with a patron group as specialized as at-risk teens, librarians will want to approach organizations that are a good fit for their library and service goals. It should be noted that although the organizations listed have a history with successful teen programming, potential issues can arise when serving youth at risk. Before brokering a partnership with an outside organization, staff should ensure the organization is both in line with the library mission and also supports the diversity of the at-risk population. A successful collaboration is contingent upon the library and its partnered

Potential Community Partners

- YWCA/YMCA
- Rotary Club
- 4-H Club
- Parent-Teacher Association/Organization
- Big Brothers Big Sisters of America
- Boys and Girls Clubs of America
- Boy Scouts/Girl Scouts of America
- Communities in Schools
- A Child's Place Inc.
- Camp Fire boys and girls
- After-school groups
- Summer camps
- Religious groups
- College fraternities/sororities

See this book's Appendix B for more information on some of these and other organizations that serve youth.

organization being in agreement regarding the needs of youth at risk and how best to serve them. Libraries will want to research youth associations and solicit support and partnerships from like-minded organizations that will be inclusive of all teens.

As with any new initiative, it is advisable to start small and also select a group that is established for the first partnership. Nothing is wrong with choosing to partner with a fledgling organization, but there is always a learning curve when partnering outside the library. Working with a group that has established policies and protocols means being able to utilize and customize their strengths and best practices to fit a new program. Regardless of the experience level of the partnering organization, it is important not to commit to more than what libraries can reasonably provide. Libraries must be realistic regarding what their staff is capable of handling and not initiate an unrealistic program. Limiting the frequency or number of commitments with a new community partner is advisable just in case the partnership is not a good fit. Then, once the commitment ends, libraries can bow out gracefully and look for another partner. If librarians find themselves in a partnership that is not working they must inform their partner and let them know in a tactful manner why the collaboration isn't working. The purpose of such partnerships is to further support services for at-risk teens and if this is not happening, library staff are within their rights to move on. When working with community partners, libraries will want to follow certain guidelines to ensure program success:

- Clearly outline the library's expectations and the partner's expectations. Agree beforehand on the mission of the partnership and how this partnership will achieve the projected mission. Write up a simple agreement and refer to it throughout the course of the program or event. The agreement does not have to be set in stone, but will provide guidance for both organizations involved.
- Locate organizations that have goals similar to the library. Find partnerships that will help represent the at-risk population and will also help endorse policies that support services.
- Compile a list of what the library can offer an organization. Library staffing and funding might be limited, but with administrator approval, partner organizations can be offered library space for meetings or be showcased on the library website or in the library newsletter.

- Collaborate with the partner organization. Do not forget that they have resources, community ties, and ideas that can help better connect the library with at-risk teens. Solicit their opinions and guidance. Learn from the benefit of their experience.
- Keep community partner(s) informed of successes with the at-risk population and always share best practices.
- Give credit where credit is due. If a library program for the at-risk population is successful because of a partnership, always acknowledge and refer to the partner when discussing the best practices and successes of the program.
- Attend community meetings and invite community organizations to library meetings. If possible, serve on a committee or board that works with at-risk teens as a representative from the library.
- Make sure to recognize community partners by always saying, "Thank you!" (YALSA, 2008)

Building a network of community partners is an excellent way to serve at-risk teens. A good partnership will help libraries stay current and keep library programs interesting to adolescent patrons. It also demonstrates that libraries care about at-risk teens and intend to include the population in future efforts.

Conclusion

Too often, perceptions of at-risk teens are negative. Library staff will want to take time to educate their colleagues and policy makers about how libraries can bridge the gap in services for these youth. Advocating for at-risk teens to be included in library policy is a solid way to ensure support. Soliciting partnerships with community organizations that are like-minded about services to at-risk teens will also assist the library mission. Do not become disillusioned or frustrated if at-risk programs are not accepted right away or if some colleagues are not supportive of new initiatives. Stay positive, and remember that library programs are not about the politics but about the teens. Libraries would be wise to invest collections and programming in young adults, who are the future voters, patrons, and tax base of their communities as working adults. If teens have a strong connection to libraries in their youth, they are more apt to see their value as adults.

References

ALA (American Library Association). 2010. *The State of America's Libraries: A Report from the American Library Association*. American Library Association. http://www.ala.org/news/mediapresscenter/americaslibraries/soal2010.

Allen, Melissa, and Amy Bradley. 2009. "Portfolios: Justify Your Job as a Library Media Specialist and the Media Budget During Times of Budget Cuts." *Library Media Connection* 28, no. 3: 48–50.

Edwards, Margaret A. 1994. *The Fair Garden and the Swarm of Beasts: The Library and the Young Adult*. Chicago: American Library Association.

Meadows, Jan. 2004. "Services Outside Library Walls." In *From Outreach to Equity: Innovative Models of Library Policy and Practice*, edited by Robin Osborne, 1–7. Chicago: American Library Association.

Spielberger, Julie, Carol Horton, and Lisa Michels. 2004. *New on the Shelf: Teens in the Library. Summary of Key Findings from the Evaluation of Public Libraries as Partners in Youth Development, A Wallace Foundation Initiative*. Chapin Hall Center for Children at the University of Chicago. http://www.wallacefoundation.org/knowledge-center/Libraries/Documents/New-On-The-Shelf-Teens-in-the-Library.pdf.

YALSA (Young Adult Library Services Association). 2008. *Speaking Up for Library Services to Teens: A Guide to Advocacy*. American Library Association. http://www.ala.org/ala/mgrps/divs/yalsa/advocacy_final.pdf.

CHAPTER 2

Understanding the Needs of At-Risk Teens

Many factors in the lives of disadvantaged teens can adversely affect their behavior both during and after adolescence. At-risk teens often must cope with neglect, abuse, boredom, and difficult living conditions. They may be unsupervised or ignored by the adults in their lives, resulting in hours of unproductive and unstructured time. Unlike adolescents who have an adult or parent taking an active interest in them, at-risk teens face an uncertain future intensified by lack of guidance and support. This neglect can place them far behind their peers academically, emotionally, and socially. Although youth at risk can benefit greatly from library services, this group is usually the hardest to reach primarily because they may not be aware of library resources, may not be encouraged to use the library, or may not even have the means to come to the library. By understanding the physical, intellectual, and emotional development of adolescents, library staff can more effectively create collections and programs that will benefit this group.

Developmental Needs of At-Risk Youth

Libraries typically define young adults as patrons between the ages of twelve and eighteen. Areas of adolescent development during this period include average cognitive, emotional, and social maturity and, according to the American Academy of Child and Adolescent Psychiatry (2011), are divided into three stages: early, middle, and late. Based on these stages of adolescent development, teens should be able to master the following as they mature into adults:

- Independence from parents, family, and childhood friends
- Ability to articulate ideas and beliefs
- Creative and career interests
- Adult sexuality and personal intimacy
- Making new connections while retaining significant personal ties

Adolescence is a time of great growth for teens as physical, emotional, cognitive, and social changes are happening at an accelerated rate. When teens grow and develop, they are influenced by factors such as their home and school environment, culture, religion, and the media. "The normal feelings and behaviors of the middle school and high school adolescent can be categorized into four broad areas: moving toward independence; future interests and cognitive development; sexuality; and ethics and self-direction" (Spano, 2004: 1–4).

The Search Institute (2012) has identified a list of "positive relationships, opportunities, competencies, values, and self-perceptions that youth need to succeed," called Developmental Assets. The organization categorizes these fundamental resources into external and internal assets. External assets are "resources imposed upon youth through family and society, such as family or neighborhood support, positive adult role models, youth programs, and a safe environment." Internal assets are "values or competencies that youth have internalized, such as achievement motivation, honesty, integrity, and self-esteem" (Brautiga, 2008: 124). The Search Institute has established that all youth, regardless of their economic or social background, require a combination of external and internal assets in order to succeed, yet far too many youth lack this foundation, especially youth at risk. In order to transition successfully to adulthood, "teens need to develop a commitment to learning, positive values, social competencies, and a positive identity" (Brautiga, 2008: 125).

Although librarians will want to be aware of average adolescent developmental stages, they must also understand that each teen is unique with a distinct personality, likes, dislikes, and comfort levels, and that at-risk development may not follow the norm. Although library services benefit at-risk teens, libraries are not the primary institutions working with them. Engaging youth at risk can be a challenge as the youth may be defensive, or they might have difficulty trusting or recognizing people who are genuinely trying to help them. Consequently, librarians serving the at-risk population are advised to defer to qualified professionals if these youth exhibit behavior that could be harmful to themselves or others. Librarians are not counselors or therapists, yet they can support teens with skills that are unique to their profession. As information specialists, librarians and staff are able to connect at-risk teens with resources designed to improve their understanding of the world and provide them with the tools to live productive lives. Ultimately libraries can create a safe and supportive environment for youth at risk, and can tailor programs and collections specifically to meet their needs.

Supporting Teen Development

Developmentally, teens need structure, yet also the freedom to explore and form their own opinions. The library is uniquely positioned to be a place where teens can access materials and technology and participate in age-appropriate activities that support their growth in a safe environment. Library services offer unique growth opportunities for teens, who are in a transitional phase of life and are quickly approaching adulthood, yet are still minors. As such, their options for independent growth and decision making are limited. Having a space to call their own where they can browse the Internet, hang out with friends, or read their favorite magazine—all for free—allows them to grow and develop into the adults they will soon become. Libraries, whether they are public, school media, or part of a youth facility, can be a haven for at-risk teens during their turbulent adolescent years.

From the standpoint of libraries, the most efficient way to support teen development is to provide services and space for teens and by extension youth at risk. However, advocates for teen services routinely must justify funds, staff time, and effort spent on a population that some believe do not have a place in libraries, particularly youth at risk. To counteract this negative attitude, supporters of teen services can point out that, if utilized properly, libraries provide powerful resources for everyone in their communities, including at-risk teens.

In many ways the library and its staff can easily meet the developmental needs of teens, yet libraries cannot facilitate teen growth if there are barriers to teen access, or if the library does not make teen services a priority. For example, there may be library staff or policies that do not make teens feel welcome; a library may have programs for teens, but they may not appeal to youth at risk; a library may not have a diverse enough young adult collection

---

Benefits of Libraries for At-Risk Youth

- "Libraries are obvious resources for help with schoolwork and pleasure reading. Book clubs, teen rooms, and materials of teen interest encourage reading and help promote a commitment to learning" (Brautiga, 2008: 124).
- Library programs can complement school learning and be a positive environment outside of the classroom by encouraging at-risk teens academically and personally.
- Support from libraries can increase at-risk teens' academic success and improve their prospects after high school.
- Library programs offer leadership opportunities to teens through volunteering, serving on youth-focused library committees, and participating in sponsored activities.
- Library programs concentrating on literacy, technology, and life skills can greatly aid at-risk adolescent development and create lifelong learners and library users.
- Libraries are one of the rare institutions that offer high-quality, free activities specifically designed for teens.
- Libraries provide opportunities for teen social engagement that create a sense of community as well as an environment that encourages self-directed exploration and learning.
- In addition to providing services, librarians act as community liaisons and have connections with local organizations, schools, colleges, and neighborhood businesses that could offer further support to youth at risk.

---

that is appealing to struggling or reluctant readers; or a library may have ample resources for teens but puts no effort into attracting and maintaining a viable teen population. In some cases, libraries may feel that they do not have the ability to offer developmentally appropriate services to youth at risk. However, many libraries are already set up to facilitate programs that are developmentally beneficial to teens.

One such example of a development opportunity is the library volunteer program. Many libraries utilize and in fact depend upon volunteers to help with the day-to-day tasks of running a library branch. In addition to adult volunteer programs, many libraries also offer volunteer opportunities to teenagers. Volunteer programs are an excellent way to harness the enthusiasm of adolescents and provide developmentally appropriate opportunities to youth in the community. "Teen volunteer programs build self-esteem, personal responsibility, and a sense of purpose while enhancing planning and decision-making skills" (Brautiga, 2008: 125). During the teenage years, youth are discovering their identities and finding their place in the world. It can be a difficult phase of life, and teens often struggle with the transition from adolescent to adult. Volunteering can help teens during their development because it "plays a major role in the formation of a person's social identity, which is shaped by one's sense of agency in collaborative efforts to make a difference in the community and the world" (Spring, Dietz, and Grimm, 2007: 16).

Volunteering at the library enables teens to work in a safe environment, gain valuable real-world experience, and contribute to their community. Teens greatly benefit from participating in volunteer programs, especially if they are considered at risk. There are numerous benefits of teen participation in volunteer programs:

- Volunteer programs help adolescents assume responsibility, yet they are still supervised and have opportunities for growth and guidance.
- Involvement in volunteer programs helps teens develop their communication and leadership skills, and gives youth a better understanding of citizenship and civic duty.
- Involvement in library programs (such as volunteering) requires teens to interact with other people who may be from different backgrounds, age groups, and beliefs, which broadens their development and awareness of world issues.
- Volunteering is an activity that helps teens gain admission to college or apply for scholarships, and also when seeking employment.
- Teen volunteers grow into adults who value their libraries and can advocate for support of libraries during tough economies or budget cuts.

Unfortunately there is a major disparity in volunteering between youth at risk and those who are from nondisadvantaged backgrounds. According to a study conducted by the Corporation for National and Community Service, at-risk teens "may be less likely to encounter volunteer opportunities, may be more likely to have other responsibilities that occupy their time, or may not live in an environment that encourages volunteering" (Spring, Dietz, and Grimm, 2007: 6). There is also "an increasing class gap in civic attitudes and behaviors; not only has there been an overall decline in civic engagement in America, but this negative trend is amplified among those from economically disadvantaged households" (Spring, Dietz, and Grimm, 2007: 1). According to the study, the majority of teens today feel there is at least a possibility that they will graduate from a four-year college. The study found that youth at risk have less confidence in the likelihood that they will graduate with a bachelor's degree. For youth at risk who volunteer, however, there is a demonstrable increase in positive social development. These teens "feel more confident that they will graduate from a four-year college, and believe that they can make a personal difference in the community" (Spring, Dietz, and Grimm, 2007: 20). The study also found that when at-risk youth do volunteer, they demonstrate the same level of commitment as those teens who are not considered at risk. Interestingly, the study showed that regardless of their economic circumstances, teens are most likely to volunteer because they are asked. Teens need and want to be of value, and it is possible for libraries to provide a meaningful experience for their teen patrons by merely asking for their help.

Libraries also support teen development by providing teens with positive adult role models. Librarians are trusted adults outside of the parent and teacher circle whom teens can approach for help with school assignments, reading suggestions, and book discussions. Library programs that are designed for teens support their development by "providing areas of interest for teens, such as reading and anime clubs, tutoring sessions, gaming competitions, computer workshops, movies, and craft programs that connect library staff with youth in a fun, constructive, and supportive environment" (Brautiga, 2008: 124). Libraries continually facilitate teen development by "encouraging teens through high expectations, constructive use of their time, and a sense of ownership" (Brautiga, 2008: 124).

To further understand the needs of youth at risk, librarians must be aware that when these teens come to the library they are looking for information, but they might also be seeking to make a connection with an adult. Creative writing instructor and Young Adult Librarian Katie MacBride, who works with teens in a detention center, states, "Don't make any assumptions. Don't talk down to teens—they'll hear it loud and clear if you do. Remember that more than anything, they have the same needs and desires as you do: they want to be respected, they want their feelings to be validated, they want to find something that makes them happy, they aren't comfortable showing vulnerability" (Katie MacBride, e-mail interview, April 18, 2011).

Teens at risk want to be reassured that someone feels passionately about their well-being and often rely on the library to help them get to the next stage of their development. Library staff who are fortunate enough to connect with youth at risk have the opportunity to provide guidance and support that can have a positive effect on the teens into their adult years. With this in mind, it is critical that libraries support adolescent development with collections, materials, and programs that are designed for use by at-risk teens.

The Facility Perspective

A wide spectrum of institutions educate at-risk youth, including public and alternative high schools, county jails, military-style boot camps, and private facilities. Some public school systems also administer educational programs inside juvenile facilities so that the residents are more in step with their peers (Clark and MacCreaigh, 2006). Many institutions housing and working with at-risk teens establish long-standing partnerships with libraries or have libraries inside their facilities. In interviewing teachers, counselors, and library staff who work with at-risk teens, we found that at-risk youth receiving library services are generally poor readers who frequently have a history of truancy that sometimes places them two to four grade levels below their peers. Usually the teens do not value reading and most likely have never completed reading a book.

Jim Britt, Lead Teacher at the Travis County Juvenile Detention Center in the Austin Independent School District in Texas, has worked with the at-risk population for over thirty years and watched many of these teens struggle with illiteracy and reading comprehension. According to Britt, "They might be able to call out words; they might be able to skim across the surface of something, but they can't really embrace the text, and they don't really read well enough to be successful at school" (Jim Britt, phone interview, September 24, 2010).

Brittany Heinrich Jarabek, formerly the Executive Director for City Youth Now of San Francisco, California, and currently Each One Reach One Assistant Director, states that many disadvantaged teens in her care lagged behind their peers academically and needed assistance to improve. Jarabek states, "Services that I personally believe are most important for these kids are the education and literacy services. They (at-risk teens) don't have a strong academic history, and all research shows that someone who is educated is less likely to fall into the traps of homelessness, poverty, violence, and illegal means of making an income" (Brittany Heinrich Jarabek, phone interview, September 17, 2010).

Even though many at-risk teens lack interest in reading, libraries working with the population have discovered that once these teens participate in a literacy-based program, they almost unanimously enjoy reading and become enthusiastic readers. "We've had many kids tell us they've never read a book until they were locked up. And once they started reading books they actually started liking them," says Britt. He added that the library is an excellent place for teens to learn a love of reading. "For many of these teens the library may be the first place they have a positive encounter with a book" (Jim Britt, phone interview, September 2010).

Juvenile institutions such as detention and foster care centers frequently introduce the concept of reading for pleasure to their residents. For many teens, no matter their circumstances, "fun" is not a word they associate with libraries, books, and reading. However, for at-risk teens in alternative schools, foster care, detention centers, or facilities with lockdown policies, reading can provide respite from their circumstances. "It's such a cliché, but they are a captive audience," says Jarabek. "When they're here they spend a lot of time in their rooms, and there's not a lot they can bring to their rooms, but they can have books at any time, so they become avid readers" (Brittany Heinrich Jarabek, phone interview, September 17, 2010).

Many facilities that serve youth at risk look to libraries to provide enjoyable reading materials for their teens that will not only keep them occupied but also enrich their lives. Additionally, the facilities want their library partners to be leaders in technology usage and to formulate technology-based programs appropriate for their charges. Whether teens come to a library program or they are participating in an outreach initiative, the schools, alternative facilities, and teen-serving organizations look to libraries to facilitate services that encourage teens' academic development. Many teen organizations and schools stress that they would like libraries to enhance their curriculum by helping to incorporate new books, technology, and literary concepts into their offered courses. These facilities want technology programs to increase teen users' skill and comfort levels by offering more than just access. Most twenty-first-century teens are adept at using cell phones, gaming systems, and computers; however, a huge gap exists between teens using technology as a convenience and utilizing it to improve their lives. Although a substantial number of teens know how to leave comments on social networking sites, most do not know how to research information for homework assignments or even fill out online job applications. Fortunately, libraries excel at offering current technology, and today's librarians are trained to give patrons hands-on experience.

Organizations also ask libraries for help in developing life skills, a frequent request that covers a broad spectrum of topics. Although libraries are not equipped to deal with every issue pertaining to the at-risk population, they are capable of offering support in certain areas. Whether in public facilities, school media centers, or juvenile detention centers, libraries can be the place where at-risk teens make their first foray into adulthood. For example, signing up teens for their first library cards and holding them accountable for fines and materials are important lessons in adult responsibility. Facility administrators point out that the teens in their care are typically better behaved in the library because they do not want to lose their library privileges. Using the library to facilitate personal growth within teens is a simple but viable way for librarians to establish rapport with this population.

The Library Perspective

"These teens just need a good book," asserts Kathleen Houlihan, Youth Program Librarian in Austin, Texas (Kathleen Houlihan, e-mail interview, August 24, 2010). This is the consensus of most librarians and library staff nationwide. Youth service librarians, school media specialists, jail librarians, and library paraprofessionals who serve at-risk teens agree that the population requires more patience and attention than the average teen but also is worth the effort. Library staff interviewed for our book cited difficulties they encountered when working with at-risk teens, including the following:

- Lack of adequate time with the teens, resulting in little or no impact on how they perceive and utilize library services
- A constantly changing population, resulting in inconsistent learning for at-risk teens
- Not knowing how to reach out to or connect with the at-risk population
- Barriers such as lack of transportation to library programs or teens living in youth facilities that do not allow programs
- Limited or no budget allocated for at-risk teen services
- Restrictions banning all materials except those deemed "appropriate"
- Lack of staff training concerning how to effectively handle this population
- Unsupportive staff or administrations that do not consider library services to at-risk youth valuable

Librarians and staff consistently struggle to encourage at-risk teens to utilize the library. Even when library services are mandated, such as in alternative education centers, many of the teens initially do not view the library as a place they want to go. Part of the problem is that some at-risk teens tend to have lower verbal performance and reading ability than their peers, plus their overall academic achievement is consistently one to two or more years below grade level. In addition, incarcerated teens have a higher rate of remaining at a grade level longer than their peers (Foley, 2001). If teens are academically low performing, they may not be inclined to utilize the library. Even if teens are high-performing students, they may not initially think of the library as an appealing place to study or hang out. Often they are not aware of current resources such as free Wi-Fi, computer access, gaming programs, or collections with popular young adult material. Overcoming the stereotype of the library being nothing more than a dusty stack of books can be a challenge for librarians wanting to engage the teen population, at risk or otherwise.

Time is also a constraint for library staff working with at-risk teens. The average stay at a juvenile facility is two to three weeks with a handful of visits to the library. A typical middle or high school has an average school year of thirty-six weeks, with students rarely visiting the library more than once a week; when they do, it is usually for less than an hour at a time. Public libraries are open year round, but with budget cuts resulting in fewer staff members, the time that librarians have to work with individual patrons is significantly less. Lack of time with their at-risk patrons is always a problem for librarians, no matter where they work. Many library staff make the most of their time with at-risk adolescents by implementing focused-area activities, updating collections, scheduling guest speakers, and constantly improving at-risk programs to make them as relevant as possible. Almost all public and school librarians want to convince disadvantaged teens that library services are beneficial and encourage them to make the library a destination in their daily lives. Likewise, librarians who work with teens in youth facilities want their patrons to use their facility library and encourage them to visit the public library once they are released. Public and school media center librarians want at-risk teens to feel at home in their facilities and to come back, hopefully, with friends.

Amy Wander, Youth Services Librarian with the Lafayette Public Library of Lafayette, Louisiana, works with at-risk teens both at the library and as part of an outreach project with the Lafayette Juvenile Detention Center. Wander has the unique opportunity to observe at-risk teens before and after they enter detention centers as well as determine how the library can best serve their needs. "Access to the library comes at a crucial time for at-risk youth. Teens see that libraries are accepting and are not here to judge them, and we have many services available to them. After participating in this (outreach) program, the teens often have a new perspective on the library, library staff, and how to utilize libraries in their own lives" (Amy Wander, e-mail interview, August 23, 2010).

Kathleen Houlihan, a youth program librarian with a public library in Texas, believes that the at-risk teens she serves are at a critical juncture in their lives, and that library resources can truly make a difference. She states, "By sharing our love of reading with these youth and inviting them to become avid readers, we give them another avenue for creative expression and exploration, as well as the self-education and lifelong learning that comes from reading. It is not too much of a stretch to realize that illiteracy is a huge barrier to gainful employment and becoming a functioning member of society. Few good choices are left to the illiterate" (Kathleen Houlihan, e-mail interview, August 24, 2010).

By encouraging at-risk teens to actively use their libraries and to seek out library services on their own, librarians and staff are aiding their development and personal growth. Introducing concepts such as reading for pleasure strengthens their literacy and academic skills, both of which will provide opportunities as they mature into adults.

"Every teen deserves a chance to have a great future no matter what circumstances are thrown at them," says Supervising Librarian–Teen Services Coordinator Pham Condello of the Ocean County Library System (Ocean County, NJ). She continues, "Sure, these teens may turn to illegal substances and activities, but it doesn't mean that their life isn't worth something. If I can help even the smallest number of teens improve their lives so they can have a better future, then I am doing my job not only as a teen services librarian, but also as a human being" (Pham Condello, e-mail/phone interview, February 22, 2012).

The Teen Perspective

What do at-risk teens think about libraries, and how can libraries meet their needs? Mr. F, a fifteen-year-old student at an alternative high school, initially declared that the library was not a place he would go. However, after attending a technology-based outreach program facilitated by the public library, he was much more interested and even wanted a library card. "I didn't know you guys had stuff for us," Mr. F said when asked why he had not used the public library before. "I knew you had stuff for adults, but I didn't even think the library had books for us." At-risk teens often believe that libraries don't have materials or services for them. When questioned, however, most of the teens we interviewed stated that libraries are valuable and that libraries in their communities are important.

When trying to meet the literary needs of at-risk patrons, librarians and staff acknowledge that teens don't always know what they want to read; they only know what they *don't* want to read. Adolescents are constantly looking for the ever-elusive "good book." They may not know what their perfect book looks like, but they can usually identify, sometimes without even opening a book, which ones aren't going to work for them. A case in point involves Mr. G, a sixteen-year-old youthful offender who likes to read only certain material. "I like books about sports, about the street, about real people, but I don't like books that are about fake people," explains Mr. G. *Tyrell* by Coe Booth has proven to be popular with many teens, Mr. G included. When he learned that the character of Tyrell was not real and could be considered a "fake person," Mr. G shrugged and replied, "Then I like books about people that *could* be real, not like fantasy people."

Many librarians and staff add that at-risk adolescents do not know what they like to read until they have tried a number of books. This appears to be true regarding all aspects of the library, from book recommendations to teen programs, and at-risk adolescents' opinions about teen-focused library programs run the gamut. Technology-based programs are consistently popular, with gaming at the forefront. Learning keyboarding and typing skills as a game also works well with many at-risk teens. However, library programs about resume writing or filling out online job applications are not as popular. Many at-risk teens acknowledge the importance of learning how to use a word-processing program but consider it boring and, for many, frustrating.

Miss J, a seventeen-year-old juvenile offender, had never typed anything other than comments on her personal social networking profile before participating in a library program teaching incarcerated teens how to create resumes. Miss J was pleased with her completed resume but did not enjoy the typing. "It was harder than I thought," she admitted. "I like computers, [and] I like working on them, but I had never really typed like that before." After the class, Miss J expressed an interest in learning keyboarding skills and was excited that her local library offered introductory classes. "I guess I'll be visiting the library when I'm let out."

Book clubs are also popular but can be challenging. Librarians who facilitate book clubs understandably want to introduce at-risk teens to classic literature such as *The Outsiders* and *To Kill a Mockingbird*, but not surprisingly the youth want to read popular and current books. Teens in a book club at an alternative high school were hesitant to read *Romeo and Juliet* but loved *Street Love* by Walter Dean Myers. "It's the same story, but I liked the newer one better," said a seventeen-year-old mother who was a resident at a teen parent shelter. "I saw myself in those characters, and I wanted to read about them."

Miss M, a pregnant sixteen-year-old living at a shelter for teen mothers, read her first book as part of a book club made possible by a partnership with a public library. Participants in the book club were allowed to keep the book and pick out a picture book for their unborn children, which motivated Miss M to sign up for the program. "I had never [finished] a book before, but I liked that we got to keep the book, and I really liked talking about it after I read it." The program also provided library card applications for the mothers-to-be and their babies, which most participants said motivated them to visit the public library and check out more books.

By demonstrating that the library is interested in fulfilling their needs, librarians show at-risk teens that they are a priority and that someone values them. Youth at risk are used to being marginalized and misunderstood by adults and even their peers. Often they are judged by their personal, economic, or social circumstances. If teens feel that library staff are judging them, whether it is true or not, they will not use the library. Library staff must be careful not to demonstrate these attitudes or else they will lose the at-risk audience. Programs that garnered the most success within the at-risk population had staff who interacted with the youth and made them feel welcome within the library. Once established with the teens, the library was more able to support youth by engaging them in intellectual pursuits and challenging them to reach their full potential. Whether libraries are public institutions, school media centers, or inside juvenile detention centers, making the facilities comfortable places for disadvantaged teens will lead them to return again and again.

No easy answer exists that defines the type of books or services that at-risk teens will find interesting. For example, although some teens enjoy books that are "fun," others want to read about "real life." Young adults serving extended jail sentences or in long-term foster care tend to prefer longer books. Many teens like books that are part of a series or by an author who has written multiple titles. Often they want to read titles that reflect their life circumstances. No matter the kind of book, teens declare that they don't want to read "boring" titles. Admittedly these examples are general, but librarians can be assured that these teens will let them know when a title is not to their liking. To clarify, Miss D, a sixteen-year-old student at an alternative high school, states that boring books always "have really ugly covers, or covers that are old, with, like, old pictures. I won't look at a book with an ugly cover." Like Miss D, many teens judge books by their covers, or library branches by their teen space, or library staff by the programs they offer. If the teens don't like what they see, they probably will not want what the library offers.

Conclusion

All at-risk teens have unique perspectives and challenges; therefore, it is beneficial for libraries to understand their developmental needs, yet treat them as individuals rather than merely part of a demographic. When partnering with an outside facility, libraries are advised to maintain an open dialogue with administrators to ensure that library and facility goals are in agreement. Keep the lines of communication open with the young adults in the facilities to find out what they want as far as library materials, and if possible, provide the requested materials. Although there is not a set of standard rules that will help libraries meet the needs of at-risk teens, the following are suggestions to consider:

- Offer opportunities for growth. A program should allow at-risk teens to expand their knowledge beyond their immediate surroundings and their current perception of themselves.
- Foster independent thought and actions. Adolescents can be afraid to speak up as individuals and often defer to the strongest person in their group. Programs requiring participants to articulate their thoughts and opinions can be challenging for teens lacking confidence, but very helpful in building their self-esteem.
- Help turn failure into success. Many at-risk teens struggle academically and are resigned to failure, so placing them in programs that allow them to be successful is important. However, they can also learn and grow from failures. Library staff can encourage disadvantaged teens not to be afraid to fail and to explore new concepts and ideas.

- Establish clear rules and guidelines and correct inappropriate behavior when necessary. All teens need boundaries and will benefit from reliable supervision. When working with at-risk teens, libraries should always follow protocol, whether in a library or at a partnered facility. At-risk teens can learn just as much from consistent rules as they can from library programs.
- Help teens focus on their future. Typically, at-risk teens lack parental involvement or any kind of adult support, which can result in their lacking guidance regarding the future. Libraries can help them look past their present circumstances and concentrate on long-term goals. Many of these young people have not considered what to do with their lives, so presenting options will help them set goals and find a positive direction.

References

American Academy of Child and Adolescent Psychiatry. 2011. "Normal Adolescent Development Part I." *Facts for Families*, no. 57. http://www.aacap.org/galleries/FactsForFamilies/57_normal_adolescent_development.pdf.

Brautiga, Patsy. 2008. "Developmental Assets and Libraries: Helping to Construct the Successful Teen." *VOYA*, June 2008: 124–125. http://www.search-institute.org/system/files/Voya+Article_0.pdf.

Clark, Sheila, and Erica MacCreaigh. 2006. *Library Services to the Incarcerated: Applying the Public Library Model in Correctional Facility Libraries*. Westport, CT: Libraries Unlimited.

Foley, Regina M. 2001. "Academic Characteristics of Incarcerated Youth and Correctional Educational Programs: A Literature Review." *Journal of Emotional and Behavioral Disorders* 9, no. 4: 248–259.

Search Institute. 2012. "Developmental Assets Lists." Search Institute. Accessed November 7. http://www.search-institute.org/developmental-assets/lists.

Spano, Sedra. 2004. "Stages of Adolescent Development." *ACT for Youth Upstate Center of Excellence Research Facts and Findings,* May 2004. ACT for Youth Center of Excellence. http://www.actforyouth.net/resources/rf/rf_stages_0504.pdf.

Spring, Kimberly, Nathan Dietz, and Robert Grimm Jr. 2007. *Youth Helping America. Leveling the Path to Participation: Volunteering and Civic Engagement among Youth from Disadvantaged Circumstances*. Corporation for National and Community Service. http://www.nationalservice.gov/pdf/07_0406_disad_youth.pdf.

CHAPTER 3

Diversity within the At-Risk Population

"At risk" is not a one-size-fits-all term, although these teens are often identified under one label. At times decision makers have the perception that at-risk teens are easily identified due to their race, socioeconomic background, and/or family life. This opinion is not entirely unfounded, as evidence shows that there is a correlation between those characteristics and certain at-risk teens. In a study facilitated by the Annie E. Casey Foundation it was found that most at-risk teens live in severely distressed neighborhoods that have high levels of four or more of the following risk factors: poverty, female-headed families, high school dropouts, unemployment, and reliance on welfare (KIDS COUNT, 1994). Although this definition is certainly valid for many of these adolescents, it is also true that more than demographics define the at-risk population. The factors and influences that place teens at risk are varied, resulting in great diversity within the population. As stated in the introduction, for the purpose of this text an at-risk teen is defined as an adolescent aged twelve through eighteen whose developmental, intellectual, emotional, educational, and information needs are not being met, potentially placing them behind their peers and hindering their successful transition into adulthood.

While libraries cannot be all things to all people, they can equip themselves and their staff to handle the diversity of the teen population through awareness, focused-area programs, developing resources for teens, and maintaining a collection that appeals to more than one type of youth. Inclusion of all teens should be the focus of libraries that truly want to reach the at-risk population.

By recognizing current issues placing teens at risk and working to make the environment of the library welcoming, libraries can be a haven offering support to a population that greatly needs it.

Factors That Place Teens at Risk

The argument can easily be made that all youth are at risk whether it be through lifestyle choices, demographics, social pressures, or family life. In reality, not every teenager is or can be considered at risk. The adolescent years are difficult for all teens from a social, emotional, and developmental standpoint. At some point in their adolescence, all teenagers struggle with a variety of issues as they grow into adults. Many teens are able to overcome these obstacles with the guidance of a parent or trusted adult, or they are fortunate enough to find the support they need through other positive connections. What places teens at risk is a lack of resources to help them navigate adolescent challenges, which in turn inhibits their successful transition to adulthood. These resources can include financial security, parental support, a stable home environment, academic encouragement, positive extracurricular activities, or access to current technology. It is highly possible for an at-risk teen to live in a two-parent household that is financially stable, yet not have adults who are involved with and actively offering guidance as they mature. It is also possible for an at-risk teen to live in a lower-income environment with limited resources, yet have supportive adults who encourage growth and development. As previously stated, at-risk teens are not limited to demographics, and from this perspective millions of teenagers across the nation grow up at risk regardless of race, sexuality, religious background, gender, or socioeconomic status. These teens are vulnerable to problems such as peer pressure, substance abuse, depression,

Factors That Can Place Teens at Risk

- Bullying
- The digital divide
- Disabilities
- Dropping out of school
- Foster care
- Gang affiliation
- Homelessness
- Actual or perceived sexual orientation
- Mental health
- Immigration
- Poverty
- Teen pregnancy or teen parenthood
- Running away from home/dismissal from home
- Substance abuse

dropping out of school, gang activity, teen pregnancy, suicide, and multiple sources of hopelessness. In terms of development, adolescence is a critical time for adults to provide guidance about risk-taking behavior. Typically, teens at risk, unlike their peers who might face the same issues, do not have a parent, guardian, or adult who can offer advice or support. It is not unusual for youth at risk to face challenges alone and not know where to seek help if they need it. The following sections cover factors that have the potential to place teens at risk.

It should be noted that teens could have more than one risk factor influencing their lives. For example, there is an unfortunate correlation between poverty and several other risk factors. Within the at-risk population, some issues go hand-in-hand, making it all the more difficult for teens to overcome the obstacles that jeopardize their future. While libraries are encouraged to use these factors as a guideline to understanding the teen population, they are also challenged to take stock of the adolescents within their own community and assess what other local factors can place teens at risk. The issues that place adolescents at risk are ever-changing, and if libraries wish to consistently serve the youth, it is their responsibility to keep aware of the problems that youth face.

Bullying

The issue of teen bullying is on the rise and crosses cultural, socioeconomic, and gender boundaries. The effects of being bullied can include a negative impact on academics, anxiety, depression, and suicidal thoughts. Teens are bullied for many reasons, such as physical appearance, socioeconomic background, perceived or actual sexual orientation, physical, emotional, or mental disabilities, or simple jealousy. Often the reasons for a teen being bullied are out of his or her control. Face-to-face bullying can and does happen every day and occurs in a variety of environments, such as in the home, in an academic setting, within peer groups, and even in public libraries and school media centers. Wherever teens congregate the potential for bullying, teasing, and harassment exists. Additionally, with the almost constant access teens have to cell phones, computers, and social networking sites, cyberbullying—or bullying that takes place in online forums—is one of the most prevalent forms of teen harassment. Being bullied can have a tremendously negative impact on the psyche of teens. According to StopBullying.gov (2012), the effects of bullying on victims can include the following:

- A higher risk of depression and anxiety
- Feelings of sadness and loneliness
- Loss of interest in activities
- Increased thoughts about suicide that may persist into adulthood
- Decreased academic achievement and school participation
- Missing, skipping, or dropping out of school
- Retaliation for harassment through extremely violent measures

StopBullying.gov also notes that adults who participated in bullying during adolescence are likely to have been or are involved in the following behaviors:

- Alcohol and other drug abuse
- Fights, vandalism of property, and dropping out of school
- Early sexual activity
- Criminal convictions and traffic citations (In one study, 60 percent of boys who bullied others in middle school had a criminal conviction by age 24.)
- Abusive behavior and aggression toward their romantic partners, spouses, or children

Teenage bullying can have serious and lasting effects. While it is certainly true that the issues mentioned here can be caused by factors other than bullying, the act of bullying can have a significant impact not only on those who are bullied, but those who bully others, and those who witness bullying.

The Digital Divide

The digital divide is a term used to describe who has access to technology versus who does not. In the context of teens, not having access to technology is a common barrier for the at-risk population. But moving beyond simple access, it is not enough to have technology and content, teens must also know how to utilize it. At a minimum, adolescents need to know how to use the technology, locate and retrieve useful information, assess the authenticity of the information, and make the findings relate to their needs (Bertot, 2003). Even if they have regular access to technology, many teens do not have the skills to utilize it and are in danger of falling behind their peers. Teens aged twelve through seventeen are the most active group of online users, with 93 percent of the teen population finding access to the Internet through computers, gaming consoles, portable gaming devices, and cell phones

(Salmond and Purcell, 2011). As of 2009, 75 percent of teens owned a cell phone. Text messaging via cell phone has become the primary way that teens communicate with their friends, surpassing face-to-face contact, e-mail, instant messaging, and voice calling as the go-to daily communication tool for this age group (Lenhart et al., 2010). Today's teens are digital natives, meaning that digital technology has always existed for them, and even more important, has been a constant presence and easily available resource throughout their lives. For twenty-first-century teens, the latest technology is prevalent both socially and academically. Outside of school, teens connect with one another through texting, gaming, social networking, and other online access points. Both in and out of the classroom, teens reap many benefits from constant access to technology, for example:

- Improved critical thinking skills
- Better understanding of and comfort level with technology
- The ability to articulate their thoughts and share opinions with peers and adults

Despite most young people's impressive computing skills, librarians will want to exercise caution when working with teens and technology. Because adolescents are often viewed as experts in technology, many adults assume that teens are able to effectively use it. However, although teens are comfortable with new technologies and able to adapt to changes more quickly than adults, at times they are not as technically savvy as adults sometimes collectively believe. For example, a teen may be able to navigate the Internet and various social networking sites with ease, yet may not know how to research a school project or even how to properly type on a computer keyboard. Although teens can have the latest in gaming or computer equipment, they may not know how to utilize it other than as a recreational device. Moreover, due to the anonymous nature of social networking and other online sites, adolescents are more apt to engage in cyberbullying because they lack the maturity to understand its consequences.

Statistics show that Internet access is highest among teens with white parents who are college educated and have an annual household income above $50,000. The facts are the same for households with high-speed or wireless Internet access, which means greater engagement in online connectivity and activities (Purcell, 2010). Those teens without ready access to technology fall far behind their peers in terms of resources and technology skills, and that can ultimately affect their educational abilities and employment potential as adults.

Disabilities

The demographic of youth with disabilities encompasses a wide variety within the teenage population. Teens can have physical, mental, or emotional disabilities that prevent them from utilizing library resources or being able to come to a library at all. The World Health Organization (2012) defines disabilities as "an umbrella term, covering impairments, activity limitations, and participation restrictions." Depending on the type of disability, teens may have a difficult time finding support. For example, although there are many programs designed for children with cognitive disabilities, there are not many comparable programs geared toward cognitively disabled teens. Teens with physical disabilities may lack the resources to engage in school activities or recreational pursuits. Budget cuts or lack of funding may limit what is provided to disabled teens. Without an advocate, teens with disabilities are at risk of developmental and social delays.

Dropping Out of School

Teens who drop out of school and do not at a minimum receive a high school diploma greatly jeopardize their future as adults. A lack of education significantly decreases their opportunities for employment, even entry-level positions. There are considerable racial gaps found for graduation rates, with students from historically disadvantaged minority groups, such as Native American, Hispanic, and African American, having little more than a fifty-fifty chance of finishing high school with a diploma, compared to the graduation rates of 77 percent for Asian students and 75 percent for white students (Swanson, 2004). Poverty and a lack of financial resources also factor into the high school dropout rate. The number of high school graduates is significantly lower in school districts with students who are eligible for free or reduced-price lunches (Swanson, 2004). Teens living in low-income families drop out of school at six times the rate of their peers from high-income families (U.S. Department of Education, 2004). High school dropouts are being shut out of professions such as skilled labor, clerical work, and related professions, which had traditionally been areas where those with less education could find employment. Even among those professions that require less skill or experience, such as jobs in retail, educational attainment is becoming more important

(Carnevale, 2001). Teens who drop out of school typically engage in high-risk behaviors such as sexual activity, crime, violent behavior, and substance abuse. There are significant financial, social, and emotional downsides to dropping out of high school, all of which hinder teens' successful transition to the adult world.

Foster Care

Teens in foster care are a vulnerable group, susceptible to risk-taking behavior because they may or may not have a consistent adult in their life, or even a consistent place to call their home. In 2009, more than one-third of the children in foster care were over the age of twelve, which averages out to 160,000 teens (Manlove et al., 2011). Teens in foster care are a broad group; they come from all racial and ethnic backgrounds, from rural and urban environments, and from a wide range of socioeconomic backgrounds. What they have in common is their adolescent age range and the fact that they are, for a variety of reasons, removed from their biological families and placed in foster care. By default, adolescence triggers a certain level of rebellion and risk-taking behavior in teens. Often the teens in foster care have been placed there due to parental neglect or abuse. These factors, combined with a turbulent home environment, can affect teens' academic performance and their involvement in school. It is not uncommon for teens in foster care to have behavioral issues or engage in risk-taking activities. Foster care can be a positive experience for teens, particularly if it removes them from an abusive situation and places them in a more stable environment. Foster care also presents challenges to teens, even if they are in the best of settings. Being in foster care often causes children to become disconnected from family, mentors, and friends (Manlove et al., 2011). Teens face difficult family, social, and personal issues when they are placed in foster care, possibly creating emotional and social barriers that they will have to work to overcome.

Gang Affiliation

Public Safety Canada's National Crime Prevention Centre (2012) found that teens who are involved in gangs tend to be from areas of society that suffer from the greatest levels of inequality and social disadvantage. Studies in Canadian and American cities facilitated by the NCPC found that youth are two to four times more likely to join gangs if they are affected by the following factors:

- Negative influences in the youth's life
- Limited attachment to the community
- Overreliance on antisocial peers
- Poor parental supervision
- Alcohol and drug abuse
- Poor educational or employment potential
- A need for recognition and belonging

Within the context of school, gang affiliation and activity can result in poor school performance, low educational aspirations (especially among young females), negative labeling by teachers, antisocial behavior, educational frustration, and learning difficulties (National Crime Prevention Centre, 2007). Without constructive guidance and support, these teens are at risk for further criminal behavior that can potentially get them incarcerated or killed.

Homelessness

There is not a current, commonly accepted definition of what it means to be a homeless teen. For the purposes of this text, a homeless youth is defined as an adolescent without a fixed residence. Reasons for teenage homelessness vary greatly and add to the confusion regarding what constitutes a homeless teen. For example, the adolescent could be part of a family that is currently homeless or in transition. Many homeless families reside in temporary shelters, utilize homeless relief programs, or stay with family members or friends until they can secure a home of their own. Families with children represent the fastest-growing segment of the homeless population (Terrile, 2009). Unfortunately, teens are as likely to be homeless and alone as with their families.

Factors such as teen pregnancy, conflicts with a parent or guardian, drug use or addiction, physical or sexual abuse, and issues with sexual orientation can contribute to teens leaving their home. Homeless adolescents lacking a fixed residence usually do not have access to basic life necessities and also are often without a safe place to grow and be a teen. This group can be difficult to reach, often avoiding shelters or programs geared toward their situation because they may be afraid of being returned to an unstable guardian, family unit, or home life. According to the National Coalition for the Homeless (2007), homeless teens are more likely to suffer from severe depression and anxiety, as well as post-traumatic stress disorder, low self-esteem, and poor physical health. In addition, as many of these teens have few legal means to earn enough money to support themselves, many turn to prostitution as a means of paying for food, money, or drugs.

Lesbian, Gay, Bisexual, and Transgender Teens

Lesbian, gay, bisexual, and transgender (LGBT) teens are a rising demographic and have become more visible in society in recent years. Many gay teens are able to find more sources of support for their choice of lifestyle with LGBT advocacy groups such as the Parents, Families, and Friends of Lesbians and Gays (PFLAG) organization, which currently is focused on maintaining the rights and safety of gay teens. Yet according to recent studies, LGBT teens are at great risk for suicide, isolation, and depression. Data clearly indicates that adolescents who are rejected by their families or peers for being LGBT were 8.4 times more likely to report having attempted suicide (Ryan et al., 2009). Bullying and harassment also put LGBT teens at risk, and, for many gay teens, the majority of the abuse takes place in an academic environment. According to Mental Health America (2012), gay teens in U.S. schools are often subjected to such intense bullying that they are unable to receive an adequate education. One contributing factor for this is that these teens may be too embarrassed or ashamed of being targeted to report the abuse; another is that teachers and authority figures might look the other way when harassment happens. LGBT students are also more apt to skip school due to the fear of threats and violence directed at them. These environments can affect LGBT teens academically, socially, and emotionally. These factors clearly place LGBT teens firmly among the ranks of young people at risk.

Mental Health

Mental health encompasses a wide array of issues that can potentially affect teens. Adolescence is always a difficult time, yet the youth of today face pressures that previous teens did not. Although it is not unusual for teens to experience social and academic stress, it is unhealthy for teens to become overwhelmed by unrealistic educational, social, family, or personal expectations. For some teens, the strain becomes too great and they can no longer cope with the pressures in their lives. According to Teen Mental Health (2012), anxiety disorders, bipolar disorders, eating disorders, depression, self-esteem issues, social phobias, obsessive-compulsive disorders, and suicidal tendencies are a sampling of common issues that can affect teens' ability to interact with adults and their peers. These issues are increasing at an alarming rate among teens and can cause an overwhelming sense of sadness, despair, or anger. Additionally, teens who are already handling issues such as living in foster homes, teen pregnancy, homelessness, gang activity, bullying, or other difficult situations are further at risk of succumbing to mental health ordeals.

New Immigrant or Non-English-Speaking Teens

A growing population exists within the United States of teens who have emigrated from different countries and seek to make a new life with their families. As the United States becomes more ethnically diverse, so do the young people aged thirteen through nineteen who make up roughly 6.9 percent of the total population. According to the U.S. Census Bureau (2011), 72.4 percent of the population of the United States is white, with the Hispanic or Latino population at 16.3 percent, African American at 12.6 percent, Asian at 4.8 percent, and Native American at 0.2 percent. In the decade since the 2000 Census, the Hispanic or Latino population has increased by 43 percent, making it the fastest-growing demographic in the United States. According to a study facilitated by the Annie E. Casey Foundation in 2005, there were 15.7 million youth in immigrant families residing in the United States. These include both children and teens born outside the United States and children born in the United States to at least one foreign-born parent. If current immigration levels continue, youth in immigrant families will constitute 30 percent of the nation's school population by 2015 (KIDS COUNT, 2007). Immigrant teens are not always made to feel welcome in their new neighborhoods, schools, or social environments. Although there are programs designed for young immigrant children, such as English as a Second Language storytimes or afterschool tutoring programs, strong support for immigrant teens does not currently exist. These adolescents face conflicts and adjustments as they transition to the United States and experience a variety of emotional and cognitive modifications to the realities of their new life. By leaving their country of origin, they leave behind a familiar language, culture, community, and social system. Potentially, they have an increased risk for psychosocial problems, school failure, drug use, and other risk-taking behaviors (James, 1997).

Poverty

According to the U.S. Census Bureau (2011), the poverty rate for children and teens under the age of eighteen increased to 22.0 percent from 20.7 percent. The poverty rate for minors was higher than the rates for adults aged eighteen to sixty-four and those aged sixty-five and older. Poverty is an issue that has far-reaching consequences for youth and can greatly affect their adult lives. The effects of poverty on children who are developing through their teenage years depend on the type, length, and conditions of the poverty. Youth who fail to make a successful transition into the labor force are at greatly increased risk of being dependent on public assistance when they become adults.

Poverty is the factor most strongly related to teen pregnancy. State comparisons show that states with higher poverty rates also have higher proportions of nonmarital births to adolescents (Moore, 1995). Teens who live in impoverished communities with high rates of welfare use and single-mother households are at higher risk for early pregnancy. "When measured against the poverty index, which accounts for family size, the typical adolescent mom and her children are significantly poorer than their counterparts" (Maynard, 1996: 14). Poverty is an issue that is, unfortunately, very common among at-risk teens, and just as unfortunately, very difficult to overcome.

Pregnancy and Teen Parenthood

Within the United States, teen birth rates remain higher than those of other industrialized countries, with teen birth rates in the United States particularly high for teens of color and those living in low-income communities (KIDS COUNT, 2006). The majority of these teens grow up in poverty and in low-income areas. They, and by extension their children, are vulnerable to further disconnection from society and to becoming entrapped in a cycle of poverty. Simply stated, teen parenthood greatly increases the risk of educational failure. Even after adjusting for race, economic status, and other characteristics, having a child before the age of twenty reduces academic achievement in the parents by almost three years. Since teen parents typically have a lower education level than their peers, they often find themselves at a disadvantage when applying for and obtaining employment. For example, if they are able to secure a job, teen mothers usually have lower wages, lower family income, and higher rates of poverty than women who give birth at a later age. Children born to teenage mothers who have not married or graduated from high school have a poverty rate of 78 percent. Comparably, the poverty rate of children born to women over the age of twenty who are currently married and/or have a high school education is at 9 percent (KIDS COUNT, 2006). According to the American Congress of Obstetricians and Gynecologists, teen fathers are less likely to finish high school than their childless peers (Martin, 2012). The

National Campaign to Prevent Teen Pregnancy (2012) notes that teen fathers earn 10 to 15 percent less annually over time than their adult counterparts who wait to have children. Teen fathers are more likely to get involved in criminal behavior, including alcohol and drug abuse, and drug dealing. Depending on their age, teen fathers can also face charges of statutory rape. Although there are programs designed to help teen mothers transition into parenthood, there is a distinct lack of programming aimed at providing assistance and education for teen fathers. Consequently, this group remains one of the more underserved within the at-risk population.

Runaway Teens

Runaway teens leave their homes for a variety of reasons. A teen might be experiencing a family crisis or come from an abusive or dysfunctional home. He or she might have school problems or social pressures that feel overwhelming. Other teens might have issues with mental illness or emotional problems or struggle with substance abuse. Pregnancy or sexual activity can cause a teen to run away. Some teens are lured away from home, such as through contact with someone through the Internet. "Throw away teens," or youth who have been abandoned, may have left their homes because their families forced them out. For others, boredom and rebellion motivate teens to run away from home (Flowers, 2001). The National Runaway Switchboard (2010) found the following:

- To earn money, nearly 35 percent of teens admitted to panhandling, the single most popular means of obtaining funds.
- Two-thirds of runaway teens report having cell phone access "some of the time."
- Over half of the teens interviewed reported that friends know where they are, while 26 percent report that parents and 25 percent report that siblings know their whereabouts.
- Thirteen percent of the teens said that nobody knew where they were.
- Over 70 percent of the teens interviewed described their leaving home as occurring on the "spur of the moment."
- Teens typically site a significant family conflict that has led to their departure.

Regardless of the reason they leave, when teens run away from their home environment they are placing themselves at risk for multiple dangers, such as homelessness, falling into prostitution, gang activity, substance abuse, sexual assault, and becoming exploited.

Substance Abuse

According to statistics from the National Institute on Drug Abuse (2012), research shows that in 2010 an estimated 22.6 million Americans aged twelve or older had used an illicit drug or abused a prescription medication, such as a pain reliever, stimulant, or tranquilizer. In many cases, teens do not start using drugs or alcohol expecting to develop a substance abuse problem. Most teens possibly see their substance use as recreational, unaware of the negative effects or the risks of becoming addicted. Unfortunately, even if teen substance abuse does not lead to adult substance use, there are still risks and consequences of even minor adolescent substance abuse. As detailed by the National Institute on Drug Abuse (2012), these negative effects can include a drop in academic performance or interest, delayed emotional development, and strained relationships with family or friends.

The biggest consequence to casual teen substance abuse is that it can develop into a true adult addiction, and very few addicts recognize when they have crossed the line. The adolescent years are a challenging time and substances such as drugs and alcohol can seem like a way to help teens cope with various pressures. However, any substance abuse, no matter how limited, can make teens vulnerable to falling into a destructive pattern of more serious substance abuse when they are adults.

Library Impact on the At-Risk Population

As will be expressed time and again in this text, libraries and their staff cannot be all things to all people. The factors that affect and shape the patrons that utilize libraries are too broad for the institution to efficiently accommodate. However, there are areas in which libraries are already well equipped to supply resources and support to those who seek it.

Libraries can directly impact the lack of technology access for many at-risk teens by, first of all, providing free computer and Internet access at their locations, and further, by offering programs on gaming, reading devices, laptop computers, MP3 players, and other technologies that might be unavailable to these adolescents. Libraries can also teach all teens responsible behavior when using technology by having a clear Internet policy and knowledgeable staff available to assist teens with technology issues, and by modeling proper online etiquette. The majority of today's teens are "digital citizens," people who participate in society using information technology. With their own access to information technology and institutional knowledge, libraries have the opportunity to grant computer access to teens, teach them how to use technology efficiently and responsibly, and show them how to have an active and positive presence online.

Because libraries are institutions that attract and offer a place for teens, they have a responsibility to be aware of the issue of bullying and provide a safe area for youth. Having a policy that supports the library as a bully-free zone is an excellent first step and can offer support to staff if an incident occurs. Facilities should also have a clear line of sight in all areas of the library so that staff can see inappropriate behavior in both supervised and unsupervised areas. Staff should also be aware of the signs of bullying and should know how to intervene before a situation gets out of control.

Librarians are not trained to be counselors, but they can easily connect teens with resources that help counteract bullying, plus they can encourage victims of bullying to report the incidents to school or police officials. Libraries and school media centers can and should hold discussions about the effects of bullying and the importance of respecting others. Also, providing materials and programs about bullying that resonate with young people, either as victims or perpetrators, can bring awareness to the issue and give patrons and students a forum for discussion. Excellent young adult literature that features bullying and its effects is available for libraries to include in their collections and provide starting points for discussion. As libraries work to engage at-risk teens and become a destination facility for them, library staff must also recognize the necessity of providing protection for teenagers and reflect that support in library policy and their YA collection.

Libraries can also offer support and representation to LGBT teens. For many gay teens, libraries are institutions where they can find information about support resources for LGBT youth and literature with gay characters. In a 2006 article in *School Library Journal*, the teens interviewed viewed their school and public libraries as "safe havens" and places to find gay-themed titles and information about themselves (Whelan, 2006). Public and school libraries are beginning to acknowledge the needs of their LGBT patrons, and with the rise in quality of teen LGBT literature, libraries have a better selection of these materials for collection development. However, the issues surrounding LGBT materials can be some of the most controversial for libraries, deterring some librarians from including materials or services for the LGBT community. In a school media setting, the Internet-filtering software that often prevents access to gay websites on student computers, combined with the lack of federal and state funding for school libraries, is also partly to blame for the inadequate services for gay teens within some schools (Whelan, 2006). Along with these obstacles, developing a LGBT collection can be a contentious issue for librarians, and one that many choose to bypass in favor of avoiding confrontation.

However, libraries having literature featuring alternative lifestyles and characters with more diversity can discourage harassment and at the same time provide teens with relatable characters. Also, book clubs and programs that feature LGBT characters can encourage dialogue between teens and promote empathy and even tolerance of different lifestyles. Librarians should be aware that a well-built LGBT collection could have an enormously positive impact on all teens and not just those who are LGBT. By offering a diverse collection, libraries can also have a positive impact on teens of difference races. Although ample data is available to support a shift in youth demographics, the number of books written about teens of color is disproportionately lower than those about white adolescents. Like any reader, teens like to read books that reflect their circumstances and what they are experiencing. Research has shown that reading achievement and reading motivation are affected by the availability of literature that offers young readers relatable stories, a view of their cultural surroundings, and insight about themselves (Hughes-Hassell, Barkley, and Koehler, 2009).

If teens do not find reading materials that interest them, they are unlikely to want to read. Within the young adult literature market, there is a persistent publishing gap regarding the ethnic diversity of teens. In the current market, the majority of YA literature focuses on white protagonists. One only has to scan the covers of books in the YA section in libraries and bookstores to see the lack of diversity, mainly due to the misconception that teens of color do not read or that they read only certain kinds of books, such as urban fiction. Librarian and blogger Amy Pattee states, "It's this belief—that teens of color don't read—as well as the assumption that those teens of color who do read need certain kind[s] of books, especially the serious and heavy stuff, that contributes to the dearth of popular fiction for those readers" (Pattee, 2011).

Teen parents can also be made to feel welcome in the library. This group can be served in two major ways: by keeping the parents connected to educational resources for themselves and by consistently exposing their children to preliteracy initiatives. Outreach is an important component when engaging this population because many teen parents do not have access to library services. For a teen parent, barriers to library services can include lack of awareness of resources, transportation issues, lack of child care, a strenuous work schedule, or attending school. Libraries can connect with teen parents by taking programs or book deposits to areas that the parents frequent and encouraging the teens to visit the library on their own time. This will require research, planning, and effort on the part of the library, but the benefits to the teens and their children are monumental. The goal of any initiative that serves teen parents should be to encourage use of the library, both for the teens and for their children. If outreach is facilitated properly, libraries can connect with two generations of library patrons, laying the foundation for library use for years to come.

The library can also offer resources to the homeless teen population. Homeless teens may come to a library or even be enrolled in school, and staff may not be aware of their situation, thinking that they are typical teenagers. The library is a logical place for homeless youth to gravitate because it is safe and clean, and has free Internet access and materials that appeal to teens. Depending on the library, there might also be free programs with activities and food. For homeless teens, the library can offer respite from their lives on the street. Library studies often focus on the negative side of the homeless patron, mainly concerned with issues such as policy, borrowing privileges, and the conduct of the patrons themselves. Many librarians are hesitant to take on what they feel is the responsibility of social services when dealing with patrons without homes. However, the issue of homeless teens and libraries does not concern policy as much as the teens' right to education and literacy. In addition to the mental and physical health issues that homeless teens face, their access to and the quality of their education is also strongly impacted (Terrile, 2009). Within the homeless teen population, a library can be the touchstone that enables these teens to stay connected and keep pace with their peers. Although libraries are not equipped to handle the social services aspect of homelessness, they are able to assist with homeless teens' information needs and can even connect youth with community resources to help them overcome homelessness.

Teens are motivated and empowered by finding books, authors, and services that reflect their life circumstances, whatever they may be. By helping ensure that teens of different backgrounds are represented, the library demonstrates leadership in literacy education, provides advocacy for adolescent diversity, and communicates to their teen patrons that they are welcome, represented, and valued.

Offering Support: Library Solutions

Although common factors are present within the at-risk population, these adolescents are more than their at-risk label, and ultimately they are still teenagers developing and moving into adulthood. Although adolescence can be difficult regardless of teenagers' backgrounds, it is particularly challenging for at-risk teens. However, through community partnerships and a strong community presence, libraries can provide useful and relevant resources for them.

An Inclusive Environment

Libraries are designed to be places where all patrons can search for a variety of information, whatever their circumstances. At-risk teens desperately need an environment where they are not judged. Regardless of the patron's situation, it is the library's job to help, not criticize. Libraries can most benefit teens by providing a safe place for them to congregate, work on homework, browse for information, use computers, or just hang out. In order to provide this kind of setting, all library staff, not just those who work with at-risk youth, must be educated about the challenges these youth face. Understanding teen diversity and factors that place teens at risk can help library staff from all areas better connect with and support this fragile population.

Information and Computer Access

For many at-risk teens, functioning in a regular academic environment can be difficult because they may be homeless or in transition, living in foster care, or dealing with school bullying, pregnancy, or any of the other factors that can place them in a complex situation. These issues can have a negative impact on them academically as well as socially. Although access to information resources and technology is something that many teens take for granted, these necessities are not guaranteed for all youth. Libraries can provide a stable environment where teens of any background or circumstance can have access to crucial information and technology. Giving at-risk teens the ability to choose what they want to read, attend programs geared toward them, and have access to the Internet for free are invaluable services to the at-risk population that libraries need to protect.

Libraries must also make it easier for teens to get online by reviewing the library Internet policy for any barriers that might prevent teens from gaining access to computer or online resources. A parental signature or proof of residence is often required to obtain a library card, but many at-risk teens may not be able to provide that information. Having a day pass or hourly pass for teen Internet use can provide access for young people without breaking library policy of not granting a permanent library card without the proper signatures. Another advantage of library use by at-risk teens is that most libraries already have Internet-filtering monitored by staff, which protects teen users from visiting sites that are inappropriate or harmful.

A Diverse and Accessible Collection

Although teens do enjoy and seek out books with topics that are familiar to them, a collection with a variety of characters, authors, titles, and themes promotes diversity, understanding, and empathy among adolescent readers. At times, the diversity of a library collection might be challenged, and in those instances it is beneficial for librarians to have a collection development policy in place that supports diverse subject matter and a book-challenging policy that allows for staff rebuttals and justification of the book's purchase. Staff can support material selection with reviews and book awards from reputable sources such as the *School Library Journal* and *Booklist*. Staff should also seek out like-minded administrators, parents, teachers, and teens who can offer support for materials that are challenged.

Along with promoting diversity, librarians should make certain that these materials are conveniently accessible to teens. Patrons should not have to go to a certain section in the library or obtain special permission to check out a book; the items they want should be easy to find and take home. Also, adding diverse titles to summer reading lists, school reading lists, or other book subject lists allows teens, regardless of their backgrounds or circumstances, to become aware of and have access to materials of diverse subject matter.

Conclusion

Libraries may not think they have a diverse teen population; however, they have no way of knowing the private issues and circumstances that are part of adolescent lives. Offering a well-balanced and varied library collection that appeals to as many teen readers as possible encourages youthful patrons to assimilate new ideas and information, as well as broadens their knowledge and worldview. Libraries that acknowledge the diversity of the teen population in their collections will attract and support at-risk adolescents to a much greater extent than a library system that chooses to ignore teen diversity.

With recent and ongoing cuts to library staff, hours, and budget, the at-risk population is losing valuable resources that are unavailable to them in other venues. Targeting the at-risk population is frequently difficult when libraries struggle with budget issues; however, youth librarians and staff must continue to support programs and services for at-risk teens lest they continue to be underserved. By providing this population with continuous access to their resources, libraries are supporting the educational, intellectual, emotional, and social development of at-risk teens.

References

Bertot, John C. 2003. "The Multiple Dimensions of the Digital Divide: More than the Technology 'Haves' and the 'Have Nots.'" *Government Information Quarterly* 20: 185–191.

Carnevale, Anthony P. 2001. *Help Wanted . . . College Required.* Washington, DC: Educational Testing Service: Office for Public Leadership.

Flowers, Ronald B. 2001. *Runaway Kids and Teenage Prostitution: America's Lost, Abandoned, and Sexually Exploited Children.* Westport, CT: Greenwood Press.

Hughes-Hassell, Sandra, Heather A. Barkley, and Elizabeth Koehler. 2009. "Promoting Equity in Children's Literacy Instruction: Using a Critical Race Theory Framework to Examine Transitional Books." *School Library Media Research* 12. http://www.ala .org/aasl/aaslpubsandjournals/slmrb/slmrcontents/volume12/hughes_hassell.

James, D. C. 1997. "Coping with a New Society: The Unique Psychosocial Problems of Immigrant Youth." *Journal of School Health* 67: 98–102.

KIDS COUNT. 1994. *KIDS COUNT Data Book: State Profiles of Child Well-Being.* Annie E. Casey Foundation. http://www.aecf.org/upload/PublicationFiles/ databook94%20file.pdf.

KIDS COUNT. 2006. "Teen Motherhood at Record Low in United States." *Data Snapshot,* no. 2 (September). Annie E. Casey Foundation. http://www.aecf.org/ upload/publicationfiles/da36221265.pdf.

KIDS COUNT. 2007. "One Out of Five U.S. Children Is Living in an Immigrant Family." *Data Snapshot,* no. 4 (March). Annie E. Casey Foundation. http://www .aecf.org/upload/PublicationFiles/snapshot_immigrant.pdf.

Lenhart, Amanda, Rich Ling, Scott Campbell, and Kristen Purcell. 2010. "Teens and Mobile Phones." Pew Internet and American Life Project. http://www.pewinternet .org/~/media//Files/Reports/2010/PIP-Teens-and-Mobile-2010-with-topline. pdf.

Manlove, Jennifer, Kate Welti, Marci McCoy-Roth, Amanda Berger, and Karin Malm. 2011. "Teen Parents in Foster Care: Risk Factors and Outcomes for Teens and Their Children." *Child Trends Research Brief*, Publication #2011-28. http://www .childtrends.org/Files/Child_Trends-2011_11_01_RB_TeenParentsFC.pdf.

Martin, James N. 2012. "Preventing Teen Pregnancy." *Pause: Your Complete Guide to Midlife Health.* American Congress of Obstetricians and Gynecologists. Accessed November 7. http://pause.acog.org/president/teen-pregnancy.

Maynard, Rebecca A., ed. 1996. *Kids Having Kids: A Robin Hood Foundation Special Report on the Costs of Adolescent Childbearing.* The Robin Hood Foundation. http:// www.robinhood.org/media/7490/khk.pdf.

Mental Health America. 2012. "Bullying and Gay Youth." Mental Health America. Accessed November 7. http://www.nmha.org/index.cfm?objectid=CA866DCF-1372-4D20-C8EB26EEB30B9982.

Moore, K. 1995. "Nonmarital Childbearing in the United States." *Report to Congress on Out-of-Wedlock Childbearing.* U.S. Department of Health and Human Services. http://www.cdc.gov/nchs/data/misc/wedlock.pdf.

National Campaign to Prevent Teen Pregnancy. 2012. "Why It Matters: Teen Pregnancy and Responsible Fatherhood." The National Campaign to Prevent Teen and Unplanned Pregnancy. Accessed November 7. http://www.thenationalcampaign .org/why-it-matters/pdf/fatherhood.pdf.

National Coalition for the Homeless. 2007. "Homeless Youth." *NIH Fact Sheet*, no. 13. National Coalition for the Homeless. http://www.nationalhomeless.org/publications/ facts/youth.pdf.

National Crime Prevention Centre. 2007. "Youth Gang Involvement: What Are the Risk Factors?" Public Safety Canada. http://www.publicsafety.gc.ca/prg/cp/ bldngevd/_fl/2007-YG-2_e.pdf.

National Crime Prevention Centre. 2012. "Identification and Operationalization of the Major Risk Factors for Antisocial and Delinquent Behaviour among Children and Youth." Public Saftey Canada. http://www.publicsafety.gc.ca/res/cp/ res/2012-iomrfadb-eng.aspx.

National Institute on Drug Abuse. 2012. "DrugFacts: Nationwide Trends—Illicit Drug Use." National Institutes of Health. Last updated August. http://www.drug abuse.gov/publications/drugfacts/nationwide-trends.

National Runaway Switchboard. 2010. "Today's Youth Want Someone to Talk to When Looking for Help." National Runaway Switchboard. http://www .1800runaway.org/media/press_releases/2010_todays_youth/.

Pattee, Amy. 2011. "It's Time for More YA for People of Color." Kirkus Reviews. http://www.kirkusreviews.com/blog/young-adult/its-time-more-ya-people-color-ya-stfu-blog/.

Purcell, Kristen. 2010. "Teens and the Internet: The Future of Digital Diversity." Pew Internet and American Life Project. http://www.slideshare.net/PewInternet/teens-and-the-internet-the-future-of-digital-diversity-3458978.

Ryan, Caitlin, David Huebner, Rafael M. Diaz, and Jorge Sanchez. 2009. "Family Rejection as a Predictor of Negative Health Outcomes in White and Latino Lesbian, Gay, and Bisexual Young Adults." *Pediatrics* 123: 346–352. http://pediatrics.aappublications.org/content/123/1/346.full.html.

Salmond, Kimberlee, and Kristen Purcell. 2011. "Trends in Teen Communication and Social Media Use: What's Really Going On Here?" Pew Internet and American Life Project. http://www.pewinternet.org/Presentations/2011/Feb/~/media/Files/Presentations/2011/Feb/Pew%20Internet_Girl%20Scout%20Webinar%20PDF.pdf.

StopBullying.gov. 2012. "Effects of Bullying." U.S. Department of Health and Human Services. Accessed November 7. http://www.stopbullying.gov/at-risk/effects.

Swanson, Christopher B. 2004. *Who Graduates? Who Doesn't? A Statistical Portrait of Public High School Graduation, Class of 2001.* The Urban Institute: Education Policy Center. http://www.urban.org/UploadedPDF/410934_WhoGraduates.pdf.

Teen Mental Health. 2012. "For Families and Teens." TeenMentalHealth.org. Accessed November 7. http://teenmentalhealth.org/for-families-and-teens/.

Terrile, Vikki C. 2009. "Library Services to Children, Teens and Families Experiencing Homelessness." *Urban Library Journal* 15, no. 2. http://ulj.lacuny.org/index.php/component/content/article/34-152/47--library-services-to-children-teens-and-families-experiencing-homelessness.

U.S. Census Bureau. 2011. *Income, Poverty, and Health Insurance Coverage in the United States: 2010,* Washington, DC: U.S. Government Printing Office. http://www.census.gov/prod/2011pubs/p60-239.pdf.

U.S. Department of Education, National Center for Education Statistics. 2004. *The Condition of Education 2004.* NCES 2004-077. Washington, DC: U.S. Government Printing Office. http://nces.ed.gov/pubs2004/2004077.pdf.

Whelan, Debra Lau. 2006. "Out and Ignored: Why Are So Many School Libraries Reluctant to Embrace Gay Teens?" *School Library Journal* 52, no. 1: 46.

World Health Organization. 2012. "Disabilities." World Health Organization. Accessed November 7. http://www.who.int/topics/disabilities/en/.

CHAPTER 4

Partnering with Youth Facilities

Partnering with a facility to serve at-risk teens is an excellent way for libraries to reach this population. Often the teens who would benefit most from library services do not come to the library, and this is especially true with the at-risk population. If at-risk teens are not venturing to the library, the library should consider going to them. Library programs at a youth facility guarantee a teen audience and also help make connections within the population. Not all youth facilities are alike, nor do they function in the same capacity, which can make them difficult for an outsider to navigate. Youth facilities housing at-risk teens are as different from each other as public libraries, academic libraries, and school media centers. Collaborating with a youth facility can be challenging, yet with preparation libraries can establish effective partnerships. Library staff will need an understanding of how the facility operates and how trends inside a facility can affect library services to teen patrons. Learning to work within the guidelines of the facility and with the facility's personnel will make the difference between a successful or unsuccessful partnership. This knowledge is just as important as any professional qualifications that librarians have and is best gained through firsthand experience.

Different Types of Youth Facilities

There are many types of programs and facilities that work with and house youth at risk. Sometimes the teens live in a facility voluntarily, sometimes they are wards of the state, sometimes they have nowhere else to go, and sometimes they are there as part of a mandatory sentence. Regardless, these teens are in an environment that is very different from their normal home, academic, and personal lives. Exploring the different types of facilities that house teens is an excellent way for librarians to connect with the at-risk community and decide what type of partnership to pursue. See Appendix B for more information on organizations that serve youth.

Alternative Schools

Alternative schools can represent many facets of the educational system. These schools can be part of traditional public schools or juvenile detention centers, or they can be stand-alone private facilities. The primary goal of an alternative school is education, but these facilities also strive to teach students life skills and give them experiences applicable to real-world situations. Often there are negative generalizations regarding teens who attend alternative schools. It might be presumed that the teens have behavioral issues or that they are a harmful influence on other students. Certainly, there are alternative schools that are designed for teens with emotional or behavioral issues. In some cases, these schools are the place where teens are sent when they are suspended from a traditional middle school or high school. However, that is not the function of all alternative schools for teens.

In some cases, teens attend an alternative school because it may be difficult for them to attend a traditional school. For example, a teen may have a learning disability and the classes in an alternative school offer more support or have more resources. A teen may be a parent and have to juggle school and the care of a child, and an alternative school provides day care while the teen attends class. A teen might have to work to help support his or her family, and an alternative school may offer more flexibility than a traditional school, allowing the teen to stay in school while working. By definition, "alternative" means "another," and for many teens these facilities offer another option that allows them to stay in school instead of dropping out.

If a library is present in an alternative school, the facility will shape how the library functions. The philosophies guiding curriculum and methodologies at alternative schools depend upon the state or region in which they are located, ranging from flexible programs of study to more militaristic and structured settings. Whether alternative schools are affiliated with public school systems or run as private institutions, curriculum and methods will differ somewhat from more traditional settings due to the needs of the students. The collections in these facilities will depend on the funding available and also on what the students are allowed to utilize.

Counseling Centers

Teen counseling centers are designed to offer support and therapy to the youth and families who need them. These centers can be private centers or can be part of a state or local organization. It is not uncommon for these centers to collaborate with other agencies that serve teens in order to offer the best support possible. Libraries may not play a direct role with teen counseling centers, yet they may work with a center if they are in the same facility or serve the same patron base. For example, counseling staff may weigh in on collection development guidelines for resources that are being used by at-risk teens. Youth counselors are excellent professionals for libraries to collaborate with regarding programs and outcomes for at-risk teens. Additionally, counseling centers can connect libraries with resources and training for library staff who wish to work with at-risk teens.

Emergency Shelters

Designed as temporary places for youth at risk to live, emergency shelters aid a wide range of teens and young adults, typically between the ages of sixteen and twenty-four. Adolescents utilizing these facilities do so for a variety of reasons. Perhaps they are dealing with homelessness or family displacement or are pregnant. They can also be runaways or young adults who lack the resources to find living arrangements on their own. Often, emergency shelters include counseling and referral services to assist adolescents with family reconciliation, or to place them in a safe environment.

The length of an adolescent's stay in a shelter depends on the shelter's rules. Since they provide short-term aid, many stipulate a maximum length of time for residency. As with other youth agencies, the setup of emergency shelters varies widely, ranging from large, dormitory-style establishments with activity rooms and meeting spaces to smaller facilities run out of personal homes. Some of the shelters are supervised by state or government agencies, while others are run as nonprofit facilities. Minors living in emergency shelters are supposed to attend school, but may not until a social service agency places them in a more permanent setting. The turnover rate in emergency centers is high, making the ability to track an adolescent's school attendance difficult.

Foster Homes

Foster care provides minors with places to live outside their homes, such as group homes, residences with relatives or with nonrelatives, or preadoptive homes. Teens can live in a variety of these settings while in foster care. For example, they may begin in a group home setting but later be moved to non-relative homes. Minors enter the foster care system at any age from infancy to eighteen, with most leaving the system once they are of legal age. In 2010, an estimated 408,425 children in the United States were in foster care, with more than a quarter living with relatives and nearly half residing in some other type of foster care (Child Welfare Information Gateway, 2012). The ultimate goal of foster care is to place at-risk adolescents in a permanent, stable environment, whether with relatives or nonrelatives. Unfortunately, a number of at-risk youth are shuffled back and forth between different types of foster care until they age out of the system. Teens in foster care typically attend traditional middle or high schools. Depending on where they are placed, they will either go to the same school they previously attended or to a new academic setting. Young people in this kind of foster care also may attend mandatory counseling or take part in programs to assist them through this transitional phase. Frequently, social service agencies are involved with placing adolescents in foster care and, subsequently, make scheduled visits to check on their progress and work with the foster caregivers.

Group or Alternative Homes

A group or alternative home is a facility for teens that is a residential, primarily nonacademic setting with adult supervision. Some group homes are public, run by state or medical agencies, while others are private, nonprofit institutions, resulting in differing philosophies and methodologies. A number of group homes accommodate adolescents and their families, while others are youth-only facilities. Adolescents can be placed within group homes because of governmental agency mandates, or because they or their families are in a crisis or transitional phase. Teens living within group homes generally go to traditional middle or high schools or attend on-site alternative educational programs. Many group home facilities also provide counseling, group and family therapy, drug and alcohol therapy, or other treatment programs. In these cases, the caregivers and counselors determine which curriculum or programs suit their charges. The length of stay varies with each institution, with some teens and families residing within group homes for a week or less, or sometimes for several months. As with foster care, the ultimate goal of these facilities is to place the teens, and teens with families, in a safe, permanent living situation.

Juvenile Detention Centers

Although the age range differs from state to state, juvenile detention centers, or facilities that hold incarcerated minors, typically hold adolescents under the age of eighteen who have either been accused or convicted of breaking the law. Because these offenders are still minors, detention staff might refer to them as "juvenile offenders," "youthful offenders," "wards," or "juvies," as opposed to "inmates" or "prisoners," as incarcerated adults are called. These centers can be independent facilities that house only minors, or they can be part of another facility such as a county jail or state prison. For many people, the terms "jail" and "prison" are interchangeable, but they are two very different entities. Jails are designed as short-term holding facilities for inmates serving sentences usually shorter than one year (although the incarceration can be longer) and for inmates awaiting trial. Prisons typically hold inmates who have been convicted and sentenced, and are long-term holding facilities. The vast majority of inmates serving time in a jail or prison are eighteen or older, although in very rare cases, a minor can be tried and convicted as an adult.

In addition to the young age of their inmates, juvenile detention centers differ from jails and prisons because educational programs are their main priority. Unlike adult inmates, juvenile offenders are required to attend classes, with the amount of time they spend in school each day regulated by the state in which they are incarcerated. Often the classes offered are set up in a similar fashion to a typical high school, making youthful offenders' reentry into regular education easier when they are released. There is an emphasis on education because juvenile detention facilities operate under the premise that adolescents in their care can be rehabilitated and returned to society as productive citizens.

Some juvenile detention centers provide a library and staff exclusively for the incarcerated population. The goal of these libraries is to offer assistance and support with schoolwork and academic pursuits and to improve teens' literacy and reading comprehension, which is often lower than their grade level. The setup of juvenile detention libraries is usually very similar to that of school media centers, and in some libraries, youth have access to additional resources such as computers. Collections and the resources the youth have access to will vary in each facility. Many libraries develop a collection with limited funds or with donations. Usually a very strict collection policy is in place that denotes the books youthful offenders have access to. Books deemed too controversial might not be found within these facilities, and many juvenile detention libraries have collections that focus on educational and workforce development.

Whether the librarians are employees of the facility or are there as part of a library partnership, they are usually allowed to provide input on collection development; however, so are educational boards, social services, counselors, and other adults working with the teens. Most if not all of the time, content of any books that the youth read must meet the guidelines set by the governing boards. Education and rehabilitation are the dominant focus of services within juvenile detention centers and unless approved otherwise, all interactions must also have that focus.

Creating Partnerships

To become an integral part of a youth facility, libraries are advised to learn the facility's routine, keep abreast of any changes in its operation, and accommodate those changes if possible. Flexibility will go far when working with a community partner that serves youth. The professionals who staff youth facilities have many demands on their time, from state and federal regulations and internal issues to handling the teens themselves, sometimes twenty-four hours a day. The majority of youth facilities have limited resources and personnel, requiring that they stretch what money and people they have as far as they can. They may reject library partnerships initially not because they do not value the services offered, but because of inadequate funds, personnel, and/or space. They may also turn down proposed library programs that appear too involved in lieu of more manageable ones. Before approaching youth facilities, it is helpful if libraries research the following:

- What type of teens does the facility serve? For example, are the teens in foster care, family transition, alternative schools, detention centers, or another facility?
- What is the staff-to-youth ratio?
- What are the operation and structure of the facility or residence like?
- What if any programs are already offered by the facility?

- What are facility policies concerning the adolescents in their care?
- What are the gaps in services that libraries can potentially fill?
- Are classrooms or meeting rooms available for programs?
- What types of programs can the facility support? For example, can it support technology or book-based activities?

Although libraries may be unable to answer all of these questions before meeting with potential collaborators, it is useful to learn as much as possible about the facility they intend to partner with. For example, a dynamic web-based program created for teens by a young adult librarian is inappropriate if the facility does not grant Internet access to its residents. The individuals running the youth facilities need to feel confident that library staff will work within their guidelines and provide services that are in the best interest of their highly impressionable young patrons or residents. Library staff who display an understanding of the facility's requirements can more easily convince administrators or caregivers that the library is a worthwhile partner.

Following Youth Facility Policies

To create and sustain a successful partnership with a youth facility, it is important that libraries follow policies to the letter. Many at-risk residents come from abusive or dysfunctional backgrounds or have grown up in physically, emotionally, and/or mentally unhealthy environments. Because many at-risk teens are vulnerable and at times volatile, most facilities and residences have strict policies governing how their own personnel and outside partners interact with the teens in their care. When librarians agree to work under these conditions, they must be prepared to adjust their programs, their demeanor, and sometimes their wardrobes before they even set foot on the premises. For all these reasons, libraries must thoroughly investigate what a prospective partner will require of library staff before embarking upon a partnership.

Partners often must go through an orientation that outlines the regulating policies before they can interact with the teens. The facility may require partners to fill out an application or submit to a background check. Some require all personnel and partners to wear a badge while inside the building or to sign in and out with every visit. During orientation, it is appropriate for library staff to bring up any questions they have about the youth facility and its residents. This will ensure that they are informed about the facility's requirements as

---

Common Youth Facility Regulations

- Dress codes forbidding potentially provocative items such as shorts, skirts, sleeveless shirts, visible tattoos or piercings, open-toed shoes, jeans, or jewelry of any kind
- Searching materials that outsiders bring into the facility (With some facilities, partners are required to bring materials in clear bags or containers so the materials are visible at all times.)
- Guidelines about physical interaction with the youth (Facilitators may not be allowed to touch young people with whom they work, including hugging or even handshakes.)
- Prohibiting electronics, such as cell phones and laptop computers
- Restricting access to pens, pencils, paper clips, and paper (To monitor what goes in and out of their buildings, youth facilities may provide partners with writing material and writing utensils for the teens.)

---

well as what is expected of them. If a facility does not give an orientation, library staff have the right to request a tour and an overview of policies and guidelines. Just as the prospective partner screens the library as a potential collaborator, the library must also screen the facility to make sure that library staff will be safe while conducting programs.

In some cases, teens may have difficulty adjusting to their circumstances inside the facility, which can adversely affect their ability to participate in programs (Wasserman, Ko, and McReynolds, 2004). It is typical for the facility to have a selection method in place to determine which teens are capable of program participation. During orientation or soon afterward, the facility should inform librarians about the process used to determine which youth will be participating in their programs and the types of programs best suited for each resident's needs. The selection responsibility should not fall on the library, yet it is appropriate for libraries to communicate how many participants a program can handle and what, if any, skill level is required. A good facility partner will listen to library staff and follow their recommendations, or at least work on a reasonable compromise. If library staff feel their classes are too large to control or the facility is not a safe environment, they should not hesitate to advise library administration to terminate the partnership. Safety of library staff as well as facility residents and personnel is paramount in any partnership, and if the facility is incapable of assuring this, the library has the right to move on to a more suitable partnership.

Your Programs, Their Facility

Before a library program can begin and staff can interact with the teens, the facility may very well want to screen and approve program content. Libraries can prepare and present an outline that details the program and projected outcomes and also list any outside equipment to be brought into the building. It is not uncommon for facilities to require program details before a partnership can be approved.

Providing programs for teens in a youth facility can be challenging for libraries, because their staff must often work within very strict guidelines. However, once a facility becomes comfortable with library services and a routine is established between the two institutions, the facility will often allow librarians more flexibility in their program options. Not all youth facilities have rigorous procedures regarding their teens and, in fact, may seek out libraries and request services to teens that they themselves cannot provide. Each facility is as unique as the teens who inhabit it. Library staff who are flexible and patient can more easily build a rapport with facility management, personnel, and residents.

If the youth facility partner is new to library services or has restrictions prohibiting online programs, book-based programs are an effective way for libraries to build a rapport with a facility. Books are easy to transport, and the facility will recognize the literary and educational merits of a book club or book deposit. However, a facility may also restrict the types of books the teens are allowed to read, including the pictures on or in the books, the types of covers (such as paperback versus hardcover), and the subjects of the books.

Library staff should not be surprised or frustrated if youth administrators or caregivers do not allow their charges access to books considered controversial. Such restrictions can feel like censorship, but facility personnel or caregivers will limit what their residents read or see based upon what they feel is appropriate. The facility may have been designated as acting guardians for the teens in their care, and library staff must respect their authority. As tempting as it might be for librarians to fight for certain materials, doing so could cause the termination of the partnership. Partnered librarians are not permanent employees and as such should adhere to the facility's rules. There is a better chance that the facility will more readily accept programs with greater diversity and content if the library adheres to program boundaries in the beginning stages of a partnership. Despite any restrictions, this is an opportunity for library staff to encourage at-risk teens to use the public library or their school media center after they are released, emphasizing that access to reading and other materials is less restricted at both places.

It is reasonable for librarians to expect the facility to allow input about their programs, including what is and isn't working. A good facility will, in fact, solicit feedback from its partners through evaluations or other assessments. Regardless of how they obtain the feedback, administrators and caregivers must be willing to listen when librarians bring up other beneficial programs for at-risk teens and current trends in teen initiatives. Librarians are, after all, innovators and leaders in the field of literacy and technology. Facility administrators should at least entertain their suggestions about potential programs that can benefit the teens in their care.

As a facility partnership develops, libraries can focus on what the emphasis of their initiatives should be, and how to maximize their time with the teens. When libraries offer teen programs in a partner facility, they should realize that limited time and class turnover are often the biggest obstacles to success. Depending on the facility, teens may only attend one or two programs before they are moved or released. Unless the facility can guarantee a consistent audience, library staff should consider having programs that can be facilitated as stand-alone activities or enhancements to established programs. More substantial programs can be offered as the partnership grows and library staff discover more efficient ways to serve the teens. No matter how much or how little time librarians spend with the facility's residents, they should view their programs as a means for encouraging at-risk teens to visit the library after their release or when they age out of the system.

Working with Nonlibrary Personnel and Caregivers

When partnering with a youth facility, librarians will interact with many of the institution's personnel or, in the case of foster care, the caregivers for the teens. Regardless of the scenario, it is important for library staff to discern who interacts with the residents and in what capacity. Depending upon the facility, these people can include the following:

- Teachers, tutors, fellow librarians
- Nurses, doctors, health care providers
- Licensed clinical social workers, counselors, psychiatrists

- Guards, officers of the law
- Religious volunteers and officials
- Maintenance crews and cafeteria crews
- Fellow community volunteers
- Residence and shelter caregivers

Every person who works or volunteers at a youth facility is dedicated to ensuring the residents' care and well-being. In an ideal environment, these individuals work together as an effective team and in the best facilities, this can and does happen. Often, facility personnel and caregivers are delighted about a library partnership and appreciate the resources that librarians bring to the teens. However, at times library staff can face difficulties in forging a working relationship with facility employees or caregivers who do not see the benefit of library services or resent the extra work associated with community partnerships. Although volunteers and partners are beneficial to youth facilities, they also require orientation, training, and supervision, all of which put increased demands on facility personnel.

To make a good start, librarians should ask to be introduced to any personnel or fellow volunteers working with the teens, or make the effort to introduce themselves. In many instances, the facility administrators or caretakers will introduce library staff to the pertinent workers. Librarians will benefit from getting to know other facility personnel, such as maintenance personnel, who have access to places in the facility that visiting partners do not. In the best-case scenario, as librarians become familiar with the facility staff, they will find associates who are supportive of library initiatives. An advocate in the facility is an excellent resource because they can represent the library during staff meetings or conferences when library staff cannot attend. Advocates will know the building, the administration, and the teens far better than a visiting partner, and can guide library staff as they become familiar with the facility.

One way to interest facility personnel in library services is to share examples of teen programming that has a product, such as a writing or digital photography class. Having the teens present their projects or displaying the projects in the facility can show the positive results of the library partnership to personnel who otherwise might not get to observe the teens. Visiting librarians can also credit the success of a program to facility staff cooperation, such as citing a helpful caseworker or detention officer who assisted with the teens. Although not every staff member of a partner facility may agree on the value of library services, it is important for library staff to express thanks and include all staff in youth progress. This can go far in smoothing the way for future interactions.

In addition to knowing who works with the teens, library staff must also understand the administrative chain of command within a youth facility. This information is useful when submitting future program or collaboration proposals. It is also beneficial for librarians to know whom to speak to regarding concerns with the teens in their programs. As stated in previous chapters, librarians are not counselors and do not have the appropriate training to handle teens who might place themselves or others in danger. If a teen's behavior is cause for concern, it is the librarian's responsibility to alert the proper staff person or caregiver immediately. It is also important for library staff to know whom to go to if they have concerns about how facility personnel are treating the teens in their care. This is not an action that should be done lightly, and librarians would be wise to have documentation of any incident they have observed that raises concern. These procedures usually are covered in facility orientation, but if they are not, librarians are within their rights to inquire about such policies. The safety and well-being of the teens are the main priorities of any library partnership.

Forming a Lasting Partnership

When libraries secure a partnership with a youth facility, it is important to ensure it is productive and meets the needs of both organizations. The facility should receive a high-quality library program that is in line with the needs of the youth in their care, and, in turn, the library reaches an underserved teen population and builds stronger ties within the community. After the first few programs have been facilitated, both agencies can evaluate the progress of the partnership. This is an excellent time to address any issues, concerns, or suggestions, or to build on best practices. If the facility wants modifications to current programs, libraries would be wise to accommodate them. Adjustments are frequently made to library programs when partnering with a youth facility, especially if the partnership is new. Often, these changes are regarding issues that haven't come up in previous discussions but were noticed once the program took place. The beginning of a partnership is an excellent time for libraries to express any opinions or suggestions and to start planning for future programs with the facility. Library staff can interview teens who have participated in the programs and get their feedback. Any pre- and post-evaluations should be shared with the facility, because they can demonstrate the outcomes of a program. As libraries move forward with a partnership, they must continue to evaluate the program to ensure that the needs of both institutions are being met, and adjust programs as needed. Appendix A provides example forms for use in evaluating the success of library partnership programs.

In case of staff turnover, procedures should always be in place at both the library and the facility. It is helpful for library staff to know of any changes in personnel or administration with their partner facility. If there is a new program director or significant administrative changes, the partnership may not continue as in the past. If there is new leadership, it is constructive for libraries to be open to new processes and approaches to programming. New leadership can inspire fresh approaches to old practices, which keeps staff interested in the programs and teen participants engaged.

Ideally, if a library staff member is leaving the initiative, the staff member taking over the position will be trained. It is helpful for the replacement to spend as much time as possible with the current staff member to learn about the program and the practices of the partnered facility. If this is not possible, incoming and outgoing staff members should arrange to meet or have a phone conversation about the youth facility partnership. These actions will help smooth the transition and maintain a good working relationship with the youth facility. If facilitated well, a change in staff is a positive thing and at times is needed to keep library initiatives fresh. For a library to maintain a lasting partnership with any facility, there must be communication and a willingness to collaborate between both parties. Most important, the teens who are participating in the programs should benefit from the efforts of the partnership.

Conclusion

At times, services and programs for youth provided by different agencies may overlap. Many at-risk adolescents can end up under the authority of a number of agencies, all of which have their best interests in mind. However, moving youth from one living situation to another can cause them to fall behind academically as well as become disconnected from society. Library partnerships can provide resources to help teens succeed in school and remain connected with their community.

References

Child Welfare Information Gateway. 2012. "Foster Care Statistics 2010." U.S. Department of Health and Human Services. http://www.childwelfare.gov/pubs/factsheets/foster.cfm.

Wasserman, Gail A., Susan J. Ko, and Larkin S. McReynolds. 2004. "Assessing the Mental Health Status of Youth in Juvenile Justice Settings." U.S. Department of Justice, Office of Juvenile Justice and Delinquency Prevention. http://www.ncjrs.gov/pdffiles1/ojjdp/202713.pdf.

CHAPTER 5

Understanding the Role of Library Staff

Working with at-risk teens can be a very rewarding experience. Librarians and staff have the ability to help these teens succeed academically, hone their technology skills, find employment or scholarships for college, and discover the great literary works of the world. When staff members work with at-risk teens, their influence goes beyond books and carries over into the development of the youth. Making a positive connection that can potentially improve a teen's life is a powerful and satisfying feeling. However, working with the at-risk population is not a calling for every librarian or staff member. Many gifted staff can and do work with young adults but have no desire to work with at-risk teens. It is important to note that not all library staff members are a good fit for the at-risk population, even if they currently work with teens. Finding the right staff to work with youth at risk is critical for the success of any library program or initiative. Although there might be a need for library services for the at-risk population, staff members must not be forced to work with this population, especially if it is outside their comfort zone. Most teens are intuitive and can sense if adults aren't comfortable with them. At-risk teens typically have fragile relationships with adults, making it important for capable library staff to interact with them.

Knowing the limits and abilities of staff is important when designing services for this population. The library's role is to provide access to information resources, facilitate age-appropriate programs, and identify and meet the needs of a traditionally underserved population. Young adult librarian and staff positions come with different criteria than those of other library jobs, requiring a combination of intuition, empathy, and institutional knowledge. When interviewing librarians and staff for this book, we found that those who work with youth at risk share many characteristics. For example, they enjoy working with teens and are dedicated to providing high-quality services to the at-risk population. Staff serving youth at risk usually work independently and often take the leadership role in young adult initiatives. They are able to assess and address the needs of their teen population and understand how library trends apply to at-risk teens. Many cultivate and maintain relationships with nonlibrary facilities, both those that serve at-risk teens and those that can benefit at-risk teens. Often programs for at-risk teens have limited or no budgets, yet the staff will find a way to provide services to their teens, even if it means using their own money to purchase supplies. They are assertive advocates of library services for at-risk teens and tenaciously seek support for the teens they serve. Dedication to the population is a resounding theme with library staff, as is demonstrating the value and need for services to youth at risk. Laura Kauffman, Special Services staff member with the Library System of Lancaster County, says this about working with at-risk teens: "I know that an early love of reading and learning can impact a future. I know even more that small successes and establishing a strong self-worth can drive [teens] to try harder, care more, and push themselves further than they otherwise could have gone. I want to help lift these teens up and turn their lives around" (Laura Kauffman, e-mail interview, February 16, 2011).

Often staff must fit in time for at-risk initiatives in an already busy schedule. The majority of staff interviewed assumed additional duties due to layoffs and budget cuts, yet still made time for outreach programs and services for at-risk teens. Following the example of staff currently serving the population, programs for at-risk teens happen because library staff pursue opportunities and advocate the necessity of services. Working with the population can present a challenge, yet for the right staff member it can be a challenge worth undertaking.

Staff Assessment: Is This Population Right for You?

To determine if the at-risk population is a good fit for staff members, it is important to know how the population relates to libraries. Libraries can be a hub for many types of teens, especially the at-risk community. It is not uncommon for runaway or homeless teenagers to make use of public library

---

Staff Assessment Questions

- Do you like teenagers?
- Do you enjoy working with teens?
- Do you feel you are easy to approach, and, if so, do you feel a teen would approach you?
- Do you feel you are patient?
- Can you work with a population that might push you outside your comfort zone?
- Are you open to working with a population in an environment that is not the library, such as a detention center or alternative school?
- Are you open to visiting environments teens frequent to encourage them to come to the library?
- When working with this population, can you remain neutral about the teen's personal history, such as arrest records, involvement in gangs, substance abuse, pregnancy, and so forth?
- Would you feel comfortable managing conflicts between adolescents?
- Can you ensure the safety of the teens who participate in your programs?
- Are you willing to spend extra time developing appropriate programs for this population, even if you have to use personal time?
- Are you flexible, willing, and able to adapt to the needs of this population?
- Are you motivated to pursue community partnerships that would benefit at-risk teens?
- Are you willing to advocate for services to the at-risk population even if no one else within your library will do so?

---

facilities because they provide access to computers and a safe place to stay. Teen gangs can also be an issue in some libraries, with gang membership higher among representative samples of at-risk youth in large cities (Thornberry, Huizinga, and Loeber, 2004). Many of the at-risk teens that library staff serve might have a history of issues such as abuse, neglect, gang affiliations, teenage pregnancy, substance abuse, or domestic violence. Because of these issues, the population can be difficult to serve, especially because libraries are cutting funding and staff services throughout the country. These facts are not meant to deter staff from working with at-risk teens but to prepare them. Understanding the factors that impact the lives of at-risk adolescents helps staff understand their roles when interacting with these young people.

Before staff members work with at-risk teens, they first must assess if the population is one they want to serve. The staff assessment questions in the above sidebar are designed to give a staff person a picture of the qualities needed when working with the at-risk population. A copy of the Staff Assessment Form can be found in Appendix A. If the answer is "yes" to the majority of these questions, then the staff member is potentially a good fit. The most important question to ask any staff member is, "Do you like teenagers?" If the answer is "No," then the search must continue for an appropriate staff member. Having experience with teens, knowledge of counseling techniques, and a background in working with the at-risk population is wonderful, but if the staff member does not enjoy being around teens, he or she will never be a good fit.

As mentioned many times throughout this text, it is important for staff to associate in a positive way with the at-risk population or the teens will not want to use the library. When asked what other qualities are needed to work with at-risk adolescents, youth services staff responded with the following:

- Staff members need to feel comfortable approaching teens and talking about current events.
- Staff members will need a good sense of humor.
- Staff members must be prepared to listen to their patrons. Teens love to talk, and they need someone to listen to them.
- Staff members will want to be familiar with current music, movies, or television shows that teens are interested in. If staff make an effort to find out what the teens enjoy, they will have common ground for building a relationship.
- Staff must act genuine with at-risk teens and not try to "fake it." If they are themselves, the young people will respect their sincerity.

As the staff members become more comfortable in their positions, they will find a method that best helps them connect with teens. Regardless of their background or experience, staff members can learn many of the skills needed to work with youth at risk through intuition and hands-on experience. Collection development and budgeting can be taught, but what can't be taught is the authentic desire to work with the at-risk population.

Librarians and Paraprofessionals: Who Is the Best Fit for Serving At-Risk Teens?

In the field of librarianship, there is a debate regarding the duties of librarians and library paraprofessionals. According to the U.S. Department of Labor, "librarian" is generally defined as a person who holds a master's degree in library science or who meets state teaching license standards for being a school librarian (Bureau of Labor Statistics, 2012a). Paraprofessionals, also referred to as "support staff" or "library technicians," are defined by the U.S. Department of Labor as staff who assist librarians in the acquisition, preparation, and organization of materials and assist users in locating the appropriate resources, but do not hold a master's degree in library science (Bureau of Labor Statistics, 2012b). In the past, there was a clear division between the tasks of librarians and nonlibrarians, yet with shrinking budgets and resources, libraries increasingly rely on paraprofessionals to help provide services to their patrons. In terms of teen services, this raised the question of who is the best fit to work with youth at risk: paraprofessionals, librarians, or a combination of both? Allowing support staff to facilitate traditional library duties is seen by some as a "deprofessionalization" of librarianship. Those who hold this view believe that a library science degree is needed because "attention to the ethical foundations of professional practice depends to a great extent on the maintenance of professional identity through a graduate education requirement and a strong professional association" (Litwin, 2009: 43–60). For others, utilizing paraprofessionals for traditional librarian roles is a wise use of library staff and library budget.

Arguments can easily be made for both positions. From the pro-librarian standpoint, librarians are professionally trained in areas such as readers' advisories, collection development, data retrieval, and information services. Current MLIS graduates are knowledgeable about technology trends and how to apply them in the context of library services. Depending on the focus of their library science degree, librarians may also have taken courses specifically designed for youth programming and teen library services. Because librarians are degreed professionals, many feel they are the appropriate staff to facilitate library initiatives and programs to youth at risk. From the pro-paraprofessional standpoint, support staff have a broad range of educational backgrounds and personal experience that can be an asset when working with at-risk teens. Some paraprofessionals have bachelor's or master's degrees that are pertinent to serving youth at risk, such as degrees in counseling or education. They may have worked with teens in previous jobs and enjoy working with the age group, or they may have an innate ability to connect with youth at risk that helps them facilitate successful programs. Paraprofessionals have the potential to serve youth at risk, especially during a time of dwindling library resources and staff.

The question of who is appropriate to serve youth at risk is unique to every library because the answer is contingent on factors such as policy, budget, staffing, and need. For example, a need might exist for service to at-risk teens, yet no librarian is interested or capable of connecting with the population. A librarian might be working with the at-risk population, but if the need is greater than what the librarian can accommodate, additional staff might be required. A library system may not have enough librarians to provide dedicated services solely to the at-risk population and a paraprofessional might be needed to work with the teens. Library policies might mandate that a degreed librarian facilitate all programming. A paraprofessional could have a skill that is beneficial for service to at-risk teens, such as speaking another language, which a librarian might not have. A library might have a strong staff of dedicated and experienced librarians who successfully work with at-risk teens, and additional support is not needed.

When assessing which staff are the most appropriate, libraries must ensure that youth are receiving quality library services that meet their information needs, regardless of who is facilitating the programs. In the new reality that is librarianship, support staff is now sharing tasks that were once exclusive to

---

Questions to Ask to Determine Who Is Appropriate for At-Risk Services

- What services do youth at risk require from the library?
- How can the library meet this need?
- Does the library have the staffing resources to accommodate the population?
- Does the library have a policy in place that defines the minimal staff requirements regarding library services? If there is a policy, does it need to be revisited? If there is not a policy, is one needed to clarify expectations?
- Are the librarians who work with (or potentially work with) youth at risk the best fit for the teen population?
- Is there training or other resources available to better prepare librarians to work with the at-risk population?
- Should the library create a youth librarian position to specifically serve teens and, by extension, the at-risk population?
- Are there paraprofessionals within the organization who could help the library meet the service needs of the teens?
- Could librarians and paraprofessionals work together to serve youth at risk?
- Can a librarian mentor a paraprofessional who wishes to serve youth at risk?
- Is the library (and by extension the staff) providing quality services to youth at risk? If not, is an adjustment in staff needed?
- Can the library see a measurable improvement in the population as a result of its efforts?

librarians. Librarians have an opportunity to utilize support staff in new and dynamic ways, potentially reaching even more youth at risk than if they were serving the population alone. Having well-trained staff who genuinely care about the teens they serve is a huge asset when working with youth at risk. Libraries may want to utilize their librarians and paraprofessionals in new and beneficial ways.

Lack of Librarian Diversity

A distinct lack of diversity exists within the field of library science. Race and language group are one indicator, yet there is also a shortage of diversity within librarians regarding age, gender, sexual orientation, economic status, and educational background. Advocacy for the at-risk population also means promoting diversity within the library staff serving youth. Libraries can only be responsive to patrons by taking into account the increasing diversity of library users when they hire staff. As noted in Chapter 3, because of the great diversity in the at-risk population, libraries must in turn foster diversity. However, the diversity of library patrons is not well reflected in its staff, schools, or professional organizations. The American Library Association's *Diversity Counts* report, which surveyed 110,000 librarians at a wide range of institutions, found that 88 percent of respondents were white and 82 percent were women (ALA, 2006). Library and information science schools report that only 11.2 percent of their students are from minority populations. For example, San José State University reported that for every one Latino librarian, there are about 9,177 Latinos in the population, compared to one Caucasian librarian for every 1,830 Caucasians in the population (San José State University, 2011). In the *Library Journal* article "The Diversity Mandate," authors Espinal and Adkins affirm that "when the profession's lack of diversity demonstrates a dissimilarity and disconnect from the nation's general population there is a professional and emotional impact on US communities. . . . Our profession loses relevance for many citizens" (Espinal and Adkins, 2004: 52–54). For many at-risk teens, the library is not a relevant factor in their lives because it does not reflect their needs or have staff they can connect with or relate to. Libraries have the potential to build a rapport with the at-risk population if they have staff who can relate to teens on levels such as ethnicity, sexual orientation, and economic background.

Many library professionals readily acknowledge the lack of diversity in the field and how it affects youth at risk. Librarian Amy Cheney, with the Alameda

County Library, Juvenile Hall, states, "The disenfranchisement of youths of color bothers me, as do the inequities that are within the library system, and the lack of diversity among librarians. We need more diversity with librarians, because librarians do not reflect the teen population at all" (Amy Cheney, e-mail/phone interview, April 25, 2011).

Reflecting the population it wishes to serve is important if libraries wish to make an impact within the at-risk community. This is not to say that librarians who are white and female cannot have a positive impact on or work effectively with the at-risk population. As stated previously, staff who care for the teens and have a genuine interest in working with them will go far within the at-risk population, regardless of their ethnic or personal background. And yet, as libraries and their staff connect with youth at risk, they must also encourage these young people to enter the library field and help create a new generation of librarians with more diversity and ethnic representation. Part of the librarian role is to connect patrons with useful resources, and the American Library Association's Office for Diversity (http://www.ala.org/offices/diversity) is an excellent source for scholarships, initiatives, and projects that promote diversity within the library field. Having a diverse staff benefits libraries tremendously because "a diverse work force makes [librarians] better stewards of the communities we serve. It enhances our ability to respond to an increasingly changing world of patrons, strengthens relations with our communities, and expands the creativity of our libraries" (Angell, Evans, and Nicolas, 2012: 45–46). In terms of services to youth at risk, diversity within the librarian population can encourage library use and inspire a new generation of library staff.

Training

All staff members need proper training if they are expected to engage or make a difference with the at-risk population. Effective service to the at-risk population begins with effective training. Professional development is essential to keep current within teen service, and part of the librarian experience is a commitment to lifelong learning.

Reading and research are the easiest and most cost-effective means to explore current issues and trends regarding the at-risk population. Exploring state library's regular publications is an excellent method to see what is happening within public and school libraries. The American Library Association's

American Libraries delivers news and information about libraries on a national scale and is part of an ALA annual membership. The Young Adult Library Services Association's *Young Adult Library Services* offers teen-focused information for YA staff. Another helpful source is the *Library Journal*, which features current news about academic and public libraries. For media specialists, the *School Library Journal* focuses on school libraries and relevant issues. Although these publications do not concentrate exclusively on at-risk teens, they contain applicable information about library services and current issues that can affect at-risk teen services. Reading popular fiction and nonfiction books for young adults is an easy way to become familiar with the different genres within YA literature. Explore what teens are checking out at libraries and buying at bookstores. Visit popular YA author websites or blogs. Also read current magazines and websites geared toward teens, especially ones that track current trends and items of teen interest. This exploration can help with at-risk program ideas and general conversation with teens.

Professional organizations are another excellent avenue for library staff to find training opportunities and to connect with like-minded colleagues. Memberships to organizations such as ALA, YALSA, and state libraries are worthwhile investments. Typically the fees for the organization also cover the cost of the association publications. Members can also take advantage of conferences and seminars, many of which have specialized presentations on teen services. Online training and webinars have been used with increasing frequency, allowing staff the chance for professional development even if they cannot attend a conference in person. Professional memberships also allow for networking opportunities with other youth services librarians who are interested in serving the at-risk population.

Finding comparable library systems and highlighting their best practices regarding at-risk teens is an effective way to educate staff about the population. Chapter 8 highlights library best practices, and readers can further research at-risk teen library services in library systems that have budgets and staffing similar to their own. For training options, library staff can invite guest speakers from another library system, youth counselors, law enforcement officers, community leaders, or representatives of youth-serving organizations to facilitate trainings, share best practices, or discuss current issues affecting the teen population. Training does not have to be limited to in-person conferences. Library staff can utilize conference calls and videoconferencing, which are usually budget-friendly options. Staff can explore any in-house training offered, as well as training offered by partnered agencies, such as city or county classes. Additionally, staff can take advantage of training outside the sphere of teen services. Many programs and ideas used for adults or children can be used for teens with a bit of age-appropriate modification. Library staff can familiarize themselves with the local teen community by visiting youth facilities, local middle and high schools, after-school programs, and community centers. Staff can approach teens and find out what they are interested in, what music they listen to, what video games they enjoy, what activities they participate in, and what they like to read. These conversations can provide a wealth of information and should be repeated as frequently as possible.

Connecting with local agencies, such as 4-H, Big Brothers Big Sisters, YMCA/YWCA, is a wonderful way to build community partnerships and is yet another resource for staff training. If a fee is attached to attending classes outside the library, explore a staff training trade-off. For example, library staff could attend training at a partnered agency in exchange for the library's offering a training workshop for that agency's employees. If funding is tight, utilizing a divide-and-conquer method of sending staff members to different training workshops and then sharing what they have learned is particularly effective for making certain that all staff receive the same training.

All staff need training in dealing with the at-risk population, whether the person in question works with disadvantaged teens or not. Libraries should establish procedures for ensuring safety in the event of dangerous circumstances surrounding a patron, especially if the patron is an at-risk teen. Working with local law enforcement and child protection agencies will help libraries establish clear guidelines, which should be included in library policies. Libraries, and by extension their staff, need to be prepared for a variety of possible scenarios when at-risk teens utilize their facility.

Just as libraries are not the lead agency for at-risk adolescents, librarians are not youth counselors and should not be placed in a position where they are responsible for the ultimate safety or well-being of their at-risk youth patrons. It is appropriate to contact a trained professional if staff believe that a teen is in an abusive situation, or if staff are approached with issues that are beyond the sphere of normal library responsibility. To clarify: When teens need assistance with information literacy, school work, or book recommendations, or come to the library to enjoy a program, this falls within what is considered normal library responsibility. However, if a teen approaches staff with a personal issue that places him or her in harm, or if staff find that a youth is in a dangerous situation, these cases fall outside of the library's jurisdiction and should be turned over to an entity that can offer help. Knowing where to refer teens if they have thoughts of suicide, suddenly find themselves homeless, have been abandoned by their parents, are involved in a gang, are victims of excessive bullying, are pregnant, or live in an abusive home environment is critical when working with the at-risk population. If libraries wish to properly serve at-risk teens, they must maintain contact with the local authorities, child protective services, homeless shelters, drug/alcohol counseling programs, and other organizations that are trained to help teens with these serious issues. Having definite procedures in place when disadvantaged teens need assistance is vital for any organization that is a hub for youth at risk. Knowing who and when to call when a youth is in danger will help teens just as much as any book recommendation or library program.

Staying Safe

By the nature of their jobs, librarians and staff are helpful and attentive and work hard to answer the questions of their patrons. A good librarian possesses excellent customer service skills and often forms a rapport with patrons that encourages continual library use. These are wonderful traits for staff to have when working with at-risk teens, who typically need as much encouragement as possible to come to the library. Staff working with at-risk teenagers may have experiences that are more emotional or intense than with standard patrons. It is not unusual for librarians to become invested in the young people with whom they work, especially if the teens come from challenging circumstances. Even so, boundaries must be observed for the safety of both the staff and the teens.

Although there is nothing wrong with building strong relationships with teen patrons, at times working with the at-risk population can blur the lines between librarian, confidante, and counselor. For any at-risk program to succeed, libraries must make certain that the young people feel cared about, listened to, and welcomed. For at-risk teens using library services, a YA librarian or staff member might be one of the few adults who try to make a genuine connection with them. Because of this, teens can sometimes misinterpret a librarian's professional attention for a personal interest. To protect themselves, staff should follow certain guidelines to maintain their safety and the safety of the teens.

Never be one-on-one with teenage patrons. Staff should avoid one-on-one time with adolescents. Always have another teen or staff member close by. This will remedy placing staff in potentially awkward or dangerous situations and will protect the teens.

Be mindful of personal contact. Many teens like to hug or are "touchy-feely." Librarians and staff members should exercise caution when teens try to hug or touch them or use any form of public displays of affection. Often, schools and detention facilities have a strict "no touching" policy, although many public libraries do not address the issue. If there is not a policy in place about personal contact, staff should use discretion when interacting with teens.

Keep personal details to a minimum. This is not to say that staff should not talk about themselves or share information about their lives. However, there is quite a difference between talking about favorite books and movies and delving into more personal topics. Many teens are curious by nature and look up to the adults in their lives as role models. Use good judgment when relaying personal information and avoid stories that are inappropriate or too personal.

Stay in control. If a program or discussion gets off topic it is perfectly acceptable to tell teens that the subject is off limits or that it is not appropriate to talk about. Lively discussion and personal revelations are encouraged when facilitating programs, but the teens are expected to stay on task, and it is the librarian's responsibility to keep activities appropriate.

Limit time with a teen if he or she becomes fixated on a staff member. If a teen tries to spend time alone with a staff member or seems fixated with a particular staff member, then the teen's interaction with that staff member needs to be limited. If possible, the staff who facilitate at-risk programs should be rotated on a regular basis. If only one staff member is available to work with these teens, he or she might try to spend an equal amount of time with each teen and not focus on only one youth. This may seem to defeat the purpose of mentoring at-risk teens; however, staff members have to remember that they are librarians, not counselors or caregivers, and must keep interaction with teens at an appropriate level.

Acknowledge "red flags." More times than not, staff members dismiss concerns about a teen's behavior toward them and feel that they are overreacting or being oversensitive when a teen does something that makes them uncomfortable. Some staff tend to ignore the signs because they may feel they are making an issue out of nothing. However, any feelings of uneasiness must not be ignored and staff should address such concerns if they arise.

Document any incident, no matter how small. There can never be too much documentation, especially concerning interaction with minors. Make sure to document any occurrence or altercation with a patron, even if it seems trivial. There may come a time later when the information is useful.

Communicate concerns with fellow staff members and supervisors. If a concern about a teenage patron arises or an inappropriate incident occurs, inform a supervisor or a person of authority immediately. If something inappropriate occurs between a minor and a librarian, the staff person should never try to handle it alone. If a situation goes awry, there is strength in numbers, and the staff member needs the support of his or her colleagues. If the incident happens at a partnered facility, the librarian needs to speak immediately with the contact person within the facility. Once again, librarians are not counselors, and if a youth under their supervision is creating an unsafe environment, the teen needs to be handled by trained professionals.

Communicate with the teen. As patrons of the library, teens are obligated to follow the rules of the facility and respect the staff. If a teenage patron breaks a library rule or acts inappropriately, he or she must be informed of it and held accountable. Arrange for a meeting with the teen and with the parents or caregivers if they are accessible. Make sure to have the support of another colleague when approaching the youth and do not try to confront the teen alone. Inform the teen of the offending issues, why the issues are inappropriate, and the consequences of their actions if they do not remedy the behavior. The goal of these meetings is to call out inappropriate behavior and reinforce the rules of the library so that the teen will not have to be dismissed or banned from the library.

Library staff must use their intuition when working with at-risk teens. If a librarian has a concern, he or she must not ignore it and should not face it alone. Sometimes there are no obvious indicators, yet a staff member might feel uncomfortable or uneasy around a certain teen, and those feelings are valid. Staff are not "bad" staff members or "bad" people if they are cautious around certain teens. Staff must also consider the other teens who utilize their services and ensure their safety. They should never ignore an uncomfortable feeling caused by a teen's behavior.

Library staff members typically have positive interactions and rewarding experiences with at-risk teen patrons. It is atypical for a situation to occur that mandates extreme measures; however, if one does occur, staff must be prepared to handle it.

Conclusion

The librarian's role is to offer support to at-risk teens through effective library services. Librarians and library staff are not youth counselors, detention officers, or social workers. Staff is not expected to know how to assist at-risk teens outside of the sphere of library services, but it is important to know where to guide youth if they are in situations that are abusive, harmful, or life-threatening. It is the responsibility of the library to prepare all staff members for potentially challenging incidents and have procedures in place for emergency situations. Interacting with disadvantaged adolescents is the only way to determine if working with them is something a staff member wants to pursue. Library staff might be interested in working with the at-risk population, but might be hesitant because they lack experience with or knowledge of the population. If offered the opportunity, staff members should observe fellow librarians working with at-risk teens to see if this group is a good fit for them. Also confer with staff at comparable library systems that facilitate programs for at-risk teens and learn what they enjoy and what they find challenging. If a staff member is considered a good prospect to work with at-risk teens, he or she should be trained by partnered agencies or within the library itself.

References

ALA (American Library Association). 2006. "American Library Association Releases National Study of Diversity in Library Workforce." American Library Association. http://www.ala.org/news/news/pressreleases2006/october2006/alalibrarydiversity study.

Angell, Kate, Beth Evans, and Barnaby Nicolas. 2012. "Reflecting Our Communities." *American Libraries* 43, nos. 1 and 2: 45–47.

Bureau of Labor Statistics. 2012a. "Librarians." In *Occupational Outlook Handbook, 2012–13 Edition*. U.S. Department of Labor. Accessed November 14. http://www .bls.gov/ooh/Education-Training-and-Library/Librarians.htm.

Bureau of Labor Statistics. 2012b. "Library Technicians and Assistants." In *Occupational Outlook Handbook, 2012–13 Edition*. U.S. Department of Labor. Accessed November 14. http://www.bls.gov/ooh/Education-Training-and-Library/Library-technicians-and-assistants.htm.

Espinal, Isabel, and Denice Adkins. 2004. "The Diversity Mandate." *Library Journal* 129, no. 7: 52–54.

Litwin, Rory. 2009. "The Library Paraprofessional Movement and the Deprofessionalization of Librarianship." *Progressive Librarian* 33: 43–60.

San José State University Library. 2011. "Facts: Minorities in Libraries." San José State University Library. Accessed April 19. http://library.sjsu.edu/librarians-tomorrow/facts-minorities-libraries.

Thornberry, Terence P., David Huizinga, and Rolf Loeber. 2004. "The Causes and Correlates Studies: Findings and Policy Implications." *Juvenile Justice* 10, no. 1: 3–19.

CHAPTER 6

Collection Development and Resources

Collection development is an important activity for any librarian because, regardless of the type of library, the collection drives the availability of materials for patron use. To develop a collection that will be appealing to youth at risk, librarians must be familiar with the mission of the library and their patrons' needs; otherwise, items they purchase will not be circulated and will waste budget, staff time, and shelf space. In the library world, the patrons' needs and interests vary widely from community to community. As a result, materials in high demand in one library might not be valued in another. At-risk teens, like other patrons, have a wide range of interests and needs. What appeals to certain teens may hold no interest for others. As such, it is important for libraries to evaluate the interests of the at-risk population when developing a collection. A helpful evaluation determines if there is a deficiency in resources and will assist in meeting the objective of fulfilling the needs of teen users.

Because the at-risk population is a growing patron base, services to these teens should be a priority for all libraries. By their own directives, a library's environment must be open and inviting to all community members. Youth at risk are no exception to this rule, and neither is the collection they will utilize. Library materials are one of the methods staff can best connect with teen users. If a library has a young adult collection that is dated or has too few copies of popular books, chances are it will not draw the interest of teen users. If a collection has current materials and items that appeal to teen readers, libraries can better engage youth at risk and entice them to utilize the library.

The titles that appeal to youth at risk may not be the same titles that libraries would initially select for the population. To produce a rich collection that is effective for youth at risk, librarians may have to balance their own notions about what they feel is right for teens with what teens actually want.

Familiarity with the budget is important when creating or updating a collection. Although this might seem like an obvious step, knowing the funds available and making a plan for their allocation will help stretch materials and their impact upon teen patrons. Many libraries also have a mission for their collection which supports the community that utilizes it. Within a library's mission, the needs of teens are often overlooked or grouped under the same policy as children's or adult services. To truly create an effective collection for teens, they must have their own defined guidelines for materials and a place within the library's overall mission statement. A well-articulated collection development policy that is inclusive of youth at risk is a powerful tool for librarians when they need to justify funds and materials for the teen population:

> A written collection development policy statement is for any library a desirable tool, which: (a) enables selectors to work with greater consistency toward defined goals, thus shaping stronger collections and using funds more wisely; (b) informs library staff, users, administrators, trustees, and others as to the scope and nature of existing collections, and the plans for continuing development of resources; (c) provides information which will assist in the budgetary allocation process. (Shaughnessy, Weber, and Dowd, 1979: 2)

Selection for a Select Population

As librarians begin the collections process, they must take into consideration where the materials will be housed and the type of teens who will have access to said resources. For example, will the collection be part of a school media center or public library with the intent to appeal to youth at risk? Will the collection be part of a youth facility such as a detention center or alternative school, or part of an outreach initiative? Are there restrictions regarding the type of materials allowed in the collection? How can the collection best serve the needs of the teens who will be using it?

The young adult literature market has skyrocketed in the past few years with the content, scope, and audience changing drastically. At-risk teens usually want materials they can relate to on topics that reflect their life circumstances. They value resources that focus on real-life challenges and serious topics, as well as entertainment. An excellent example of a genre that is appealing to at-risk teens is "street fiction." Street fiction, also known as street literature, urban literature, gangsta lit, hip-hop lit, or ghetto fiction, is a depiction of the harsh realities of living in the ghetto or poorer neighborhoods and the daily dealings of crime, poverty, hustling, gangs, prostitution, incarceration, drugs, and other urban elements (Guerra, 2010). This particular genre captures environments and life situations that are familiar to many youth at risk. "The young adult street literature genre is slightly gentler than its adult counterpart, but still contains significant language, violence, sex, drugs, crime, and other elements that characterize inner city living" (Guerra, 2010: 3–4). Although street fiction is extremely popular with teens, it is highly controversial among librarians, educators, parent groups, and the public. The critics feel that the genre glorifies the criminal lifestyle, features sexist depictions of women, and promotes negative stereotypes of urban neighborhoods, and in particular, negative stereotypes of people of color. Supporters argue that street fiction is creating huge numbers of new readers and the genre can be used to encourage teens to try different titles once they have become interested in street fiction. There are many issues and controversies surrounding street fiction and it can be difficult to justify inclusion of the titles in a school media center or public library, much less in youth facilities with teens "who are in custody for some of the very issues the books address" (Guerra, 2010: 4).

The street fiction genre is a perfect example of what teen readers want and what educators usually want to avoid. However, teen readers are not easily deterred from controversial titles, and in fact, seek them out. A group of teens participating in a library outreach program cited notorious titles such as Melvin Burgess's *Doing It*, Lee Childs's *A Child Called It*, Coe Booth's *Tyrell*, and Sistah Souljah's *The Coldest Winter Ever* as the books they most wanted to read. Even outside of street fiction, there are many titles that could be viewed as being too advanced for adolescent readers, or even inappropriate. Once again, knowing where the materials will circulate and the population who will be utilizing the materials is an essential component of any collection development process and particularly beneficial when serving at-risk teens. Ultimately, libraries want a collection that is devoured by teens, not ignored.

At-risk teens are like other teens when it comes to reading. They appreciate reading content they can relate to. Their interest is in areas that either enhance their lives or speak to their personal experiences. To engage an at-risk teen in reading, the library must have a collection that appeals to their literary needs. As such, the evaluation of library material for at-risk teens must be placed within a broader evaluative scale of a library's collection:

> Libraries often find themselves feeling pressure to evaluate themselves without really knowing specifically what needs to be evaluated. Assessment should always be designed to provide information about the collections or services you provide in order to direct how well our library is fulfilling its mission. The mission guides the assessment, and the assessment results help shape future goals. Assessment results help keep goals outcome oriented. (Baird, 2004: xi)

Selecting materials for at-risk adolescents can be a challenge for libraries because of constraints in budget, materials, and space. In some cases, the administration making the decisions may not have an interest in or see the value of providing library materials to an at-risk population. Traditionally, many of the titles and materials that are of interest to these youth deal with controversial subjects such as gangs, teen pregnancy, sex, substance abuse, and other "real-world" situations that some administrators, regardless of the facility, wish to keep their teen readers from encountering. In addition, if a library is partnering with or part of a youth facility, that institution may require the library to abide by strict guidelines regarding the types of materials the teens read. Consequently, librarians must be knowledgeable about the population for whom the collection is being designed, what if any limitations will be placed on the collection, and where and how the materials will circulate.

Developing Public Library and School Media Center Collections

Developing a collection for at-risk teens in a public library or school media setting can help increase the diversity of library materials and the readers who use them. It's often assumed that all teens have access to books through their school libraries, but this is only true for the teens who actually attend school. At-risk teens in urban or low-income neighborhoods may not have school media centers or access to these resources outside of a school environment. They also may not have access to, or be aware of, public library resources. A partnership between public libraries and school media centers can more effectively help close the gap of access that occurs within the at-risk population. School media specialists and public librarians can easily work together to assess the quality and quantity of their individual collections and combine efforts to establish a worthwhile collection for teens in their community. As an added bonus, librarians can cross-promote programs, materials, and services to reach previously inaccessible adolescents. Because every teen population and library is different, it is important for library staff to assess the specific needs of their residents and develop policies that provide the most effective services:

> Libraries should identify the long and short-range needs of their clientele, and establish priorities for the allocation of resources to meet those needs. A collection development policy statement is an orderly expression of these priorities and they relate to the development of library resources. (Shaughnessy, Weber, and Dowd, 1979: 5)

Perhaps the most important aspect of collection development for libraries to consider is the needs and reading interest of their particular at-risk population. Surveys are an excellent way to find out what subjects attract these teens and how the library can provide the materials. Before gathering any information, it is important to establish which teens to survey and how to use the responses. To collect the widest array of responses possible, librarians will want to gather information from teens both inside and outside their library. If partnering with a youth facility or community group, libraries will naturally want to obtain permission to give the survey to the teens. If a library does not have a partner facility, the librarians can approach schools, after-school programs, and community organizations that work with teens. Often these institutions are happy to help develop other resources for the teens in their care as long as the teen responses are kept anonymous. If librarians are adventurous and want the most current sampling of what interests teens, they can venture into areas where teens can be found, such as shopping malls, fast-food restaurants, recreational parks, and home neighborhoods. Librarians can also consult with teachers, counselors, social workers, and community agencies that serve youth at risk to gain an understanding of the educational, developmental, and emotional needs of the teens. Those in the youth services field might also have recommendations about book titles that focus on specific issues putting teens at risk, such as eating disorders, suicide, bullying, or abuse. The more diverse the response to a collections survey, the better sampling librarians will have of at-risk teens' interests and needs.

When creating the survey, librarians must remember that the assessment is about the teens, not the library. General questions such as "What do you want from your library?" or "What do you like to read?" will probably not garner a worthwhile response because teens may not know what they want their library to provide. Because the goal of the survey is targeting at-risk teens who don't use the library, librarians may have more success with questions that ask for specific interests and likes and dislikes of the teens. The following are examples of potential survey questions:

- How do you like to spend your free time/What do you do for fun?
- What TV shows/music/movies do you enjoy?
- Who is your favorite performer/actor/musical artist?
- What websites do you go to?
- What magazines do you read?
- What video/online games do you play?
- What social networking sites do you use? (e.g., Twitter, Facebook, You-Tube, etc.)
- What are your favorite smartphone apps?
- Where do you like to go shopping?

Effectively utilizing the information gathered is the next step in collection development. While some responses may sound inconsequential, they actually give librarians a sense of what teens find appealing and want to learn more about. If teens are enthusiastic about gaming, they may want to read books about web design or creating digital content. If teens draw or enjoy art, libraries may want to purchase more titles that demonstrate how to draw or use artistic techniques. Often librarians create collections based upon their personal knowledge about a certain title or upon its reputation as an award-winning or "classic" text. Although there is nothing wrong with this method, librarians must remember that usually teens quite literally judge a book by its cover. It is not uncommon for a teen to pass over the award-winning titles for the more eye-catching, popular items. The results of a teen survey offer snapshots of topics that currently interest youth and can greatly help librarians purchase materials appealing to the at-risk population. As with all collection development, survey information will become dated and will need to be collected again periodically in order to keep materials up-to-date and appealing to teens. Adolescents typically enjoy having the opportunity to give their input to adults; librarians should not have difficulty gathering information as long as the survey focuses on teen interests. Finally, surveys benefit both the library and at-risk population by offering the opportunity for librarians to interact with the teens and establish a library presence with these youth.

Once a collection has been purchased, librarians need to market it to at-risk patrons. This does not mean that the library should have a section labeled "Books for At-Risk Teens." On the contrary, the library should work to incorporate titles for at-risk teens into the general collection. Setting up appealing, face-out displays is an excellent way to catch the attention of teen patrons, regardless of the demographic. Intriguing labels such as "Books for Bad Boys," "Stories from the Street," "Fast Reads," and "Girl Power" can draw teens to certain titles and increase circulation. In all probability, these displays will also appeal to the majority of adolescents, providing an excellent way to justify budget and staff time. If budgets allow, library staff also should try to incorporate materials other than books into the collection for at-risk teens. The following are items to consider:

- Periodicals
- Graphic novels and manga
- Audiobooks and Playaways
- DVDs and CDs
- Digital media downloads

Because many patrons still purchase DVDs and CDs, librarians might continue to purchase those formats for the time being. However, an increasing number of teens have access to electronic devices and computers, enabling them to download digital items. Along with traditional materials such as books and periodicals, librarians will want to establish a digital collection for their young patrons. Offering downloadable content is an effective means of keeping youth interested in library services. As streaming and downloading options become more common, patrons can and will access movies, music, and books in a digital format. To engage their teen population, eventually libraries will need to offer these resources to their patrons.

Downloadable e-books are an excellent way to appeal to tech-savvy teens. An e-book, also known as an electronic book or digital book, is a text-and-image-based publication in a digital form produced on, published by, and readable on computers or other digital devices (Suarez and Woudhuysen, 2010). E-book reading devices can be found on patrons' cell phones, computers, or on reading or computing tablets. The publishing world is constantly developing its e-book content, adding new titles almost daily. Examples of e-book providers that serve public libraries and school media centers include the following:

- NetLibrary (http://www.netlibrary.com/). NetLibrary, which is part of EBSCO Publishing, is an electronic content provider of audio-books and e-books through their website that primarily serves libraries. Libraries control the content available in their portal by purchasing content from NetLibrary. Materials are viewable online or as a protected PDF.
- OverDrive (http://www.overdrive.com). Overdrive is a digital distributor of downloadable e-books, audiobooks, music, and video titles. The company's core business is the management of digital content for publishers, libraries, schools, and retailers.

When developing their collection, it is important for librarians to work toward providing an appealing array of materials for their at-risk patrons. Access to materials such as books, audiovisual items, and digital content is an excellent way to increase teen patronage and engage at-risk teens.

Developing Collections for Youth Facilities

When working with at-risk adolescents, librarians may have the opportunity and responsibility to develop a library collection for a youth facility. These facilities can include alternative schools, foster homes, detention centers, youth shelters or hostels, or any organization that serves or houses teens. The librarian might be a full-time staff member at the facility, a librarian from a public or school library partner, or even a volunteer from the community. Whatever the circumstances, developing a collection for at-risk teens in a youth facility can be a challenge but can also be a rewarding experience for librarians.

A youth facility library typically has a different focus for its patrons than a public library or school media center. Often the materials in a youth facility primarily focus on educational support or workforce development in addition to leisure reading materials. Librarians in this setting will want to consult facility administration and craft a material selection policy for their teen patrons. If the facility does not have a preexisting policy for collection development, policies from a comparable library can be used as a template and modified to fit the youth facility. Like those in public or school libraries, this policy will act as guidelines for librarians when creating a collection of appropriate reading materials for the facility's residents. When developing these policies, librarians would be wise to include the facility administration and also counselors, social workers, jail guards, teachers, and any other personnel who interact with the teens. This will help round out the policies and also potentially head off any issues that could result in the challenging or removal of library materials after they have been purchased. Including other personnel can also help librarians recruit supporters within the facility for the library collection and services for teens.

Selecting materials for a youth facility can be a difficult and time-consuming project. There may be more directives placed on the content that can be purchased or even admitted in to the facility. Because youth facilities often act as guardians of the minors in their care, administrators can determine and restrict the materials and programs to which the teens have access. See the sidebar on page 98 for an example of what facilities guidelines can look like.

Although librarians can and should promote materials for their at-risk teen patrons, they must abide by the rules of the facility when developing a collection. To avoid disputes and provide the best possible collection for teens, libraries are advised to put together a collection policy that clarifies standards for materials of the collection. This action establishes guidelines and provides support for librarians' decisions should a challenge arise. A second advantage of a collection policy is that librarians can revisit and amend it as needed, offering flexibility as the library's needs change.

Another action similar to one public and school librarians already undertake is evaluating the characteristics of the teen population residing in youth facilities. These facilities serve a wide array of teens with different needs, so librarians will need to put together a collection that will benefit every type of patron. For example, a collection for male juvenile first-time offenders will look different than a collection for pregnant adolescent mothers. Librarians can also evaluate the environment where teens access the materials. Do the teens come to a library setting or does the library bring items to the teens? Are the teens allowed to browse for books within their library, or do they make selections from materials pulled for them? Every group (and subgroup) of at-risk teens will have slightly different needs, so librarians should research each group in order to identify what the patrons require from the library.

In order to promote understanding of the collection and to prevent potential censorship of titles, librarians will need to express to facility decision makers that the materials selected are intended to be rehabilitative and positive in

Sample Restricted Materials Guidelines
for Youth Facilities

Publications that may not be distributed include but are not limited to those which meet one of the following criteria:

- They depict or describe procedures for the construction or use of weapons, ammunition, bombs, or incendiary devices.
- They depict, encourage, or describe methods of escape from correctional facilities, or contain blueprints, drawings or similar descriptions of the same.
- They depict or describe procedures for the brewing of alcoholic beverages, or the manufacture of drugs.
- They are written in code.
- They depict, describe, or encourage activities which may lead to the use of physical violence or group disruption.
- They encourage or instruct in the commission of criminal activity.
- They contain sexually explicit material which by its nature or content poses a threat to the security, good order, or discipline of the residents.
- They contain homophobic, pornographic, obscene, or sexually explicit material or other visual depictions that are harmful to students.
- They use obscene, abusive, profane, lewd, vulgar, rude, inflammatory, threatening, disrespectful, or sexually explicit language.
- They use language or images that are inappropriate in an educational setting or disruptive to the educational process.
- They contain information or materials that could cause damage or danger of disruption to the educational process.
- They use language or images that advocate violence or discrimination toward other people (hate literature) or that may constitute harassment or discrimination or create a serious danger of violence in the facility.
- They depict the martial arts.
- They depict tattooing. (Guerra, 2010)

nature. This may be the most difficult aspect of collection development for a facility that houses youth at risk because many titles that appeal to these teens can be perceived as controversial or inappropriate.

Librarians, of course, will not want to purchase materials that may trigger a teen's regression to illegal or inappropriate activity. Titles that promote drug addiction, glorify gang involvement, or glamorize illegal activities are not appropriate for teens trying to change past behaviors. However, librarians will also want to communicate to administrators that young adult literature includes many titles of excellent literary quality capable of resonating in a positive manner with at-risk teens. Carefully selected young adult literature can encourage discussion among these teens about contemporary issues and promote self-awareness about their day-to-day decisions and life choices. See the sidebar for resources for at-risk teen collection development.

Although it is true that certain titles focus on controversial subjects, librarians need to convey to the administration that these titles also contain positive messages of redemption, hope, and personal growth. "The best of this literature may have sexual content, but it does not demean women. It may have violent content, but it does not glorify violence. It may address gangs and drug use, but it does not romanticize either. It may be about people of color in difficult situations, but it is not racist" (Guerra, 2010: 8). A thoughtfully developed collection will demonstrate to facility administrators how to engage youthful readers with materials that attract them while also make discerning choices based on the requirements of the facility and the populations they serve.

> ### Resources for At-Risk Teen Collection Development
>
> Librarians can gain administrative support by having administrators read the titles or synopsis of titles that are being selected for purchase. Show administrators book reviews from reputable sources, such as *Booklist* or *VOYA*. If an author has a website, direct administration to view it and find out the background behind the material. Share statistics about how literacy helps with recidivism rates and preventing youth incarceration. Resources such as *Reading and Writing Quarterly,* the *Remedial and Special Education Journal,* and the Office of Juvenile Justice and Delinquency Prevention are good places to look for current trends and statistics to support library programs and collection policies.

Maintaining a Mobile Collection

A mobile collection is an excellent way to establish a library presence within the at-risk community. Although it takes time to select, transport, and trade out the items, the value of making library materials available to at-risk teens usually outweighs the effort expended by offering librarians the opportunity to reach these adolescents. However, because mobile collections typically serve nontraditional readers who may or may not have a library card or ever set foot in the library, materials are somewhat different than in a permanent library collection. In addition, this type of patron may make library administrators hesitant about the idea of a mobile collection because of concerns about library items not being returned. If this issue arises, librarians can remind administrators that sometimes items checked out from a library branch by "regular patrons" are not returned either.

Libraries are built on the model of lending materials with the expectation of their return, and borrowing rules regarding a mobile collection should be no different than those for a library branch collection. Library staff facilitating a mobile collection must be clear with borrowers concerning the library's expectations for treatment of library materials, how to check out new items, and how to return them. Adolescent borrowers, like adults, must be held accountable for the items they check out from a mobile collection just as they are if they check out an item from a public library branch or school media center.

If a library has a deposit collection at a youth facility, the library will want to first formulate a policy for checking out and returning items that works for both the facility and the library, and then decide on a method of operation. If the library has the means to remotely check out items, or if library staff can check out the items once they return to the library branch, they can issue library cards to the teens in the facility. Another option is to assign a facility staff member to be in charge of the collection as well as checkout and return responsibilities. The library will have to decide what works best for its program and what the facility can accommodate.

Although budget constraints affect both mobile and branch collections, librarians face unique challenges when setting up mobile collections. First of all, the amount of materials capable of being transported in a mobile collection, such as in a bookmobile, is limited. A bookmobile collection usually encompasses patrons of all ages, not just teen patrons, so librarians must carefully select items that will appeal to and make the most impact upon the population. When putting together a mobile collection for at-risk teens, there are several factors to consider:

- *Classic titles versus popular titles.* Librarians are constantly faced with having to decide whether to purchase items for quality or quantity. The latest popular titles typically have high circulation, but eventually they lose appeal as patrons move on to the next fad. Classic titles have a longer shelf life but can invoke little interest in teens. When making selections for a mobile collection, try to create a streamlined version of a branch collection, one that provides a good mix of popular and classic materials.

Including both popular items and familiar classics is a practical choice for a mobile collection and one that offers a good selection for teen readers.

- *Hardcover versus paperback.* This can also be a quality versus quantity issue due to budget limitations. Paperbacks are less expensive than hardcovers, but the shelf life for paperbacks is significantly shorter, especially for popular items. Although hardcovers more often appeal to librarians, many teens prefer paperback books because of their smaller size, portability, and glossy covers. In order to learn what items are the most attractive to mobile collection patrons, make note of the items left on the shelves. If teens check out most of the paperbacks but few of the hardcovers, it is easy to determine the type of materials the teens will want.
- *Series versus stand-alone titles.* Paperback books and serials go hand-in-hand in the collection process. Many serials are printed as paperbacks and are extremely popular with teen readers. However, borrowers will be frustrated if a mobile collection does not offer the complete series or if books in the series are continually checked out. When possible, include complete popular series for teens, and if some of the series' books are perpetually off the shelves, it is the perfect opportunity to encourage teens to visit their local library.
- *Books versus alternative formats.* Consider offering patrons a mix of materials. In addition to carrying books, offering periodicals and audiovisual items will enhance a collection and greatly interest teen borrowers. At times, a mobile collection is limited to a book-only selection, especially if used as a deposit collection for an off-site facility. However, if having a variety of formats is an option, librarians are encouraged to include an array of items. Since a mobile collection is a condensed version of a library branch collection, library staff can strongly advocate for alternative formats, especially when the items interest teens.

As with any activity involving the at-risk population, librarians will need to thoroughly assess the needs of the teens being served. Those with a deposit collection in a youth facility ought to consult with administrators and staff about what types of items are needed and ask the teens what types of books they would like to read. In addition, when visiting at-risk communities outside youth facilities in the bookmobile, librarians need to ask patrons what they would like to check out, and on the next visit try to have those materials available. Mobile collections can reach adolescents who have never visited the library and can also encourage at-risk teens to become regular library users. Having a diverse mobile collection for teens can raise the library's visibility and impact on the entire community and encourage at-risk teens to visit the library on their own.

Selection Tools

When creating a collection for the at-risk population, librarians can use a mix of traditional selection tools, surveys of the population, and intuition about what will appeal to teen patrons. Although there is tremendous diversity within the at-risk population the majority of teen materials target the white, middle-class market. These titles, while popular, do not represent the typical at-risk population or even the average teen population. Librarians can best serve the at-risk population by working to provide diversity within a collection and materials that teens can truly identify and connect with. Currently there is not a library review source for materials such as teen magazines, movies, or popular music. For the time being, librarians will have to conduct personal research or network with colleagues when purchasing these materials. Several established review journals are a mainstay for collection librarians who are conducting a search for books to purchase:

- *Booklist.* Published by the American Library Association, this magazine provides over 8,000 reviews of books, audiobooks, reference sources, videos, and DVD titles each year. There is a section devoted to young adult materials, and librarians might find the selection of adult material reviews useful as well.
- *School Library Journal* (http://www.schoollibraryjournal.com/). This resource has an excellent website in addition to its print material. SLJ reviews materials for public libraries and school media centers and provides insight into the latest books, graphic novels, films, games, technology, and teen trends. For young adult librarians, there is *SLJTeen* (http://www.schoollibraryjournal.com/csp/cms/sites/SLJ/Info/SLJSLJ TeenSubscribe.csp), a free e-newsletter that provides information about teen content, and the blog Adult Books 4 Teens (http://blog.school libraryjournal.com/adult4teen/) that gives a monthly selection of adult books that appeal to teen readers.

- *VOYA* (*Voice of Youth Advocates*, http://www.voya.com/). This library magazine "serves those who serve young adults." VOYA provides a diverse evaluation of teen fiction, nonfiction, graphic novels, and other various genres. It also provides booklists, reviews, and recommendations written by librarians and by teens. With six issues a year, this publication provides excellent guidance for young adult librarians.

Networking with fellow librarians who serve youth at risk is an excellent way to keep tabs on what interests teens. Along with review journals, there are electronic discussion lists that focus solely on teen materials and their appeal to the young adult market. YALSA-Lockdown (http://lists.ala.org/wws/info/yalsa-lockdown) is one such example. This list is an open discussion between librarians and staff who primarily serve and work with incarcerated youth, whether the teens are in a juvenile hall, group home, treatment center, and so forth. Collection development is a popular topic, as well as library policy, programs for at-risk teens, and general discussions about teen issues. Many of the topics discussed can be applied to at-risk teens in general and not only to the incarcerated population. The YALSA-BK (http://lists.ala.org/wws/info/yalsa-bk) list is another excellent electronic discussion list for collection development. Focusing on book discussions and suggestions for purchase, this group discusses specific titles as well as general collection issues. Subscribers also will gain access to YALSA's Best Books for Young Adults, Popular Paperbacks, and Quick Picks for Reluctant Young Adult Readers.

The YALSA selection lists and award winners are also a good resource for librarians and provide a starting point for a collection. Librarians will want to research the recommendations carefully and purchase what is relevant to their patron base, because the titles focus on general teen readers and not just the at-risk population. Amazon.com has a well-organized section for teen readers with new and notable books and popular genres and titles. Beneath many of the titles are links to author websites, interviews, and book trailers. Reviews are posted by professional journals as well as readers, many of whom are teens.

Along with these selection tools, librarians need to continuously ask the teens what their reading interests are and do their best to accommodate them. Surveys, exit interviews, book evaluations, and reviews from the teens are extremely beneficial for the collection development process and give the best picture of what the teen population wants to read, and what will bring them to the library.

Conclusion

As libraries develop their collection for at-risk teens, it is important to remember that it is a progression, not a one-time event. The needs and tastes of the adolescent community evolve just as they do for adult users. Librarians must continue to weed and update the collection if they want to keep teens interested and engaged in library services. Strive to offer teen patrons a collection of materials with a range of subjects, characters, backgrounds, and settings. A good collection will allow teen patrons to find themselves in the materials available and identify with the books. In addition, do not assume that the at-risk population likes to read only one type of genre or about one subject matter. The goal of the collection is to represent what teens want to read while introducing them to new material and concepts.

References

Baird, B. J. 2004. *Library Collection Assessment through Statistical Sampling*. Lanham, MD: Scarecrow Press.

Guerra, Stephanie. 2010. "Reaching Out to At-Risk Teens: Building Literacy with Incarcerated Youth." *PNLA Quarterly* 75, no 1. http://unllib.unl.edu/LPP/PNLA%20Quarterly/guerra75-1.pdf.

Shaughnessy, T., H. Weber, and S. Dowd. 1979. *Guidelines for Collection Development*. Chicago: American Library Association.

Suarez, Michael Felix, and H. R. Woudhuysen. 2010. *The Oxford Companion to the Book*. Oxford: Oxford University Press.

CHAPTER 7

Technology Programs and Resources

The teens of today live in a world where technology is readily available and part of their everyday lives. For many teens, access to technology is as simple as utilizing a personal computer, cell phone, or gaming unit, or making use of the equipment within an academic environment. A 2010 study conducted by the Kaiser Foundation found that today's youth on average spend seven hours and thirty-eight minutes per day consuming media, with the majority of it being music, television content, computer/online content, and gaming (Rideout, Foehr, and Roberts, 2010). The ability to effectively utilize technology is one of the most essential skills that teens can acquire, affecting pivotal social indicators such as academic accomplishment and future career earnings. "Understanding the role of media in young people's lives is essential for those concerned about promoting the healthy development of children and adolescents, including parents, pediatricians, policymakers, children's advocates, educators, and public health groups" (Rideout, Foehr, and Roberts, 2010: 2).

As discussed in previous chapters, the digital divide is unfortunately prevalent within the at-risk teen population, preventing many disadvantaged teens from learning how to effectively utilize information technology and keep pace with their peers. A variety of barriers prevent youth at risk from having access to and training with information technology. The teens in question might not have a computer or Internet access at home. Their schools, libraries, and academic environments might have inadequate technology labs and classes due to budget cuts. The teens might be in a state of transition, such as in foster care or in a youth shelter, where access to technology is minimal. Or, the teens might be in a detention facility or alternative education center where technology access is strictly prohibited. "Teens from lower-income families are less likely to own cell phones or computers, buy things online or use Web sites for news or information than teens from wealthier families" (Vahlberg, 2010: 14). Interestingly, even with these barriers, at-risk teens are "more likely to use online social networks, keep a blog or go online to seek health information than wealthier teens" (Vahlberg, 2010: 14).

Whatever the reason, this gap in service to the at-risk population affects the teens from an educational and social standpoint. Teens who do not have access to information technology and adequate training in how to use it are less prepared to compete academically, while those who have access to and use of information technology are expected to increase their employment and earning potential. Effective use of information technology can help young adults with researching and locating employment and also prepare teens to successfully compete in a job market where an increasing number of employers require such skills and offer higher wages as compensation (Eamon, 2004). As teens transition into adulthood, the ability to successfully use technology is a skill that librarians can help develop, especially among the at-risk population.

Libraries face numerous challenges in bringing quality technology programs and access to youth at risk, such as budget cuts, reduction of staff, and less time for outreach. Despite these challenges, libraries are still uniquely positioned to meet the needs of the at-risk population because of their highly trained staff and the resources within their facilities. Libraries can provide free Internet access for teens, databases for research, homework help, and free technology classes. In an outreach capacity, having focused partnerships within the community that target at-risk youth can help libraries meet the technology needs of this population. A technology outreach program does not have to be ongoing or have a large budget to be successful. Many free sites that patrons and libraries have ready access to can help promote library programs within the at-risk community. Social networking sites, such as Facebook, Twitter, or YouTube, allow libraries to connect with teens online and showcase programs and services to teen users. According to a 2011 study by the Pew Research Center, "Social media use has become so pervasive in the lives of American teens that having a presence on a social network site is almost synonymous with being online. Fully 95% of all teens aged 12–17 are now online and 80% of those online teens are users of social media sites" (Lenhart et al., 2011). An online presence can make it easier to reach teen populations, because teens can access social networking sites from personal computers, cell phones, or other devices. Additionally, library staff can access social networking sites for outreach efforts at any location that can provide an Internet connection.

Libraries can make a powerful impact by having programs that focus on the positive development of technology skills. "Today, libraries are places where reading meets hands-on learning and where quietness coexists with voices and music. The latest advances in technology for children and teens, specifically, robotics sets and media-rich software, are bringing new challenges and opportunities for lifelong learning" (Romero, 2010: 17). As detailed in this chapter, ample programming opportunities exist for librarians to educate teens about safe and effective use of technology. With creativity and a bit of effort, librarians can meet the technology needs of the at-risk population and provide quality services that the teens might otherwise be denied.

Starting a Technology-Based Program

Starting a technology-based program for at-risk teens can be daunting, but with planning and experimentation, librarians can create quality activities that will greatly enhance the teens' experiences with the library. The following are tips that librarians might consider before starting a technology program with at-risk youth:

- Find out what the teens are interested in or where their knowledge base is regarding technology. Do not make assumptions about the technology level of the teens. If partnered with a youth facility, work with administrators to ascertain the technology needs and skill levels of the youth. If facilitating a program within a library, develop simple assessment questions for the teens, which can give a baseline for where to begin.
- When working with another facility, make sure they understand exactly how the technology will be used and why. A demonstration and presentation that aligns program goals with the facility's objectives can smooth the way for librarians to carry out proposed activities.
- Have a practice session or "dress rehearsal" with the technology to be used for the program before the program begins, even with familiar software. The teens' first impression of the library should certainly not be that the computers do not work, or that the librarian does not know

how to work a program. If presenting a program in an unfamiliar facility, testing equipment on-site before the program begins is wise. Otherwise, be prepared for potential problems.

- Keep a checklist of equipment that needs to be available, everything from backup batteries to an extension cord. Also, keep program notes that detail successes and challenges, which can help staff better facilitate any future programs. (Kelly Czarnecki, Teens and Technology Education Librarian, Charlotte Mecklenburg Library, personal communication, April 7, 2011; all material in this chapter attributed to Czarnecki is from this communication)

It will also be important for library staff to gain support for their programs long before they actually try to implement a technology-based initiative. Regardless of the audience, facilitating a technology program can take effort and staff time. Implementing a technology-based program to youth at risk within a library branch is very different when doing so with a partner facility. Staff will need to gain the support of their colleagues, administrators, and partner facility before the implementation of any technology program. Some suggestions for librarians follow:

- Create a program outline and timeline for the project. What are the goals for the project, what skills will the teens learn?
- Ask fellow tech savvy colleagues to review the project plan. They may be able to assist with defining the outcomes and benefits of the program, or help with the initial planning.
- Know the details of the technology that is being used, how it will be implemented, and be prepared to answer questions about it. Be prepared to explain to library administrators and community partners about the program in detail. For example, will the program require Internet access? Will participants need any special skills? How will the finished projects be accessed or displayed? What will this cost in staff time and equipment use? Staff who can answer questions quickly and thoroughly will be better positioned to garner approval for their program. If staff does not know the answer, find out in a timely manner. (Nelson and Braafladt, 2012)

Utilizing technology-based programs with youth at risk is an excellent way to encourage the population to use the library. Library staff who desire to utilize technology with their teens are referred to the three Ps of technology-based programs: planning, preparation, and practice.

Promoting Literacy through Technology Use

Technology services to at-risk teens can be facilitated in a variety of settings, and librarians can use different tools to train teens in the use of information technology. Understanding how to facilitate these programs can be overwhelming, and seeking the support of colleagues who have experience with the at-risk population can help library staff who are new to technology services facilitate successful programs.

One such resource is Kelly Czarnecki, the teens and technology librarian at ImaginOn: The Joe and Joan Martin Center in Charlotte, North Carolina. Czarnecki has been a public librarian for over eight years and has worked with the homeless population for over fifteen years. She has written numerous articles about her work with teens and technology and has spoken nationally and internationally on the topic, including at the American Library Association conferences on several occasions. She writes a monthly column for the *School Library Journal* and *Gaming Life*. Her published works include *Gaming in Libraries* (part of THE TECH SET), and *Digital Storytelling in Practice: Library Technology Reports*. Most important, Czarnecki has ample experience facilitating technology programs to youth at risk, both in a public library setting and with partnered facilities.

Czarnecki states that in the twenty-first century, "Understanding and being able to use technology is an essential skill encompassing more than just knowing how computer hardware and software operate. Being technologically literate involves being able to apply technology tools in ways that will improve collaborative skills to produce effective results. Teens must also use critical thinking skills to solve problems and analyze situations in order to create new ideas more effectively. All young people today, at-risk teens included, must learn how to develop these skills in order to succeed in life."

Typically, teens who are at risk read at a lower grade level than their peers. A common mind-set among some librarians regarding at-risk teens and technology use is that before the teens are allowed to use a computer, they should first know how to read and comprehend a book at their reading level. According to Czarnecki, this is a misconception; although it is true that many at-risk teens do read below the level of their peers, the act of reading, comprehending, analyzing, and organizing information is not merely limited to words on paper. With the widespread availability of computers, words on a screen can integrate and enhance the elements of information literacy in exciting ways for teens who struggle to read. For example, being able to collaborate online, whether through typed comments, blog posts, or auditory feedback, can open up at-risk teens to a much richer and deeper understanding of the world around them. Creating a digital story by interweaving sound, images, text, and video can be a gateway for many at-risk teens to comprehend such skills as sequence, expression, and critical thinking in ways that, for them, far surpass reading a book.

"If libraries and youth facilities make teens with lower reading levels wait until they can read at grade level before exposing them to technology skills, they will only continue to be further behind their peers," says Czarnecki. In her book *Teens, Technology, and Literacy; or, Why Bad Grammar Isn't Always Bad*, Linda Braun examines the definition of literacy, particularly how it relates to technology. Braun points out that the primary definition of literacy is to read and write. However, she acknowledges that the definition of the word leaves a lot of questions such as "to read and write what?" (Braun, 2007: 4). Over the past several decades, the influence of technology—from cell phones to instant messages to social networking—has dramatically changed the way that society reads, writes, and communicates. The definition of what it means to be literate has changed as well, opening up new possibilities of communication and expression for teens.

Braun goes on to say that looking at literacy as only "school knowledge," or as a skill that can only be measured and indicated as a factor in school achievement implies that "the world in which the learner lives . . . does not have any relevance to how literate he is" (Braun, 2007: 7). Czarnecki states that although the ways in which teens communicate with each other, such as texting via cell phone or sharing music online, may not seem related to literacy, the fact that youth are using technology to communicate is important and should be encouraged. Libraries, and by extension their programs, are the perfect learning centers "to develop, test, and offer educational technology programs for youth that are grounded in key literacy skill building . . . which fill those critical out-of-school-time hours" (Nelson and Braafladt, 2012: 5).

Librarians have the opportunity to integrate educational technologies into at-risk teens' communication, which can in turn support their reading and writing development. However, far too often this support does not occur because library staff might feel that the teens will misuse the tools, or that their lower reading level limits their ability to use the technology. These concerns are another barrier to service to the at-risk population, and one that is unfortunately facilitated by certain library staff. Librarians who have doubts about the capabilities of at-risk teens would do well to remember that all technology users must start their training at some point, and that patrons learn best with hands-on experiences. Technologies such as audiobooks, e-books, library databases, desktop publishing, and multimedia composition are important forms of literacy that teens, especially those who are at risk, can benefit and grow from. As their horizons expand, so will the opportunity to increase avenues of learning through new friends and mentors beyond the harmful influences they possibly have been exposed to closer to home.

Czarnecki demonstrates an excellent example of teen development through technology with a variety of outreach programs facilitated with male youthful offenders in partnership with the Mecklenburg County Sheriff's Office. Czarnecki frequently utilizes Teen Second Life, a free online community where participants use avatars to interact, to demonstrate information technology concepts to at-risk teens. In a Second Life program facilitated by Czarnecki and library staff, the youthful offenders and staff were on an "island" in the virtual world of Teen Second Life, participating in a workshop to develop a community project. The primary means of communication was typing messages online, with the exchange meant to be short sentences such as "Hi, how are you?" Several of the teens agonized over forming "the perfect sentence," minding their grammar and spelling before hitting the enter key. Communication was hindered because pauses between messages were too long. Staff explained to the youth that this was an informal conversation and that the teens should not be concerned about perfecting their grammar, but to answer as best they could and enjoy the experience. According to Czarnecki, when the youth stopped trying to perfect every sentence, their comfort level with the technology vastly improved. In addition to instant messaging, the participants also learned about the different forms of online communication and how some scenarios, such as blogging or e-mail, might call for a more formal expression, while chatting online allowed for more relaxed communication. The program allowed the teens to develop the kinds of skills that are difficult to quantify, such as knowing what type of communication to use when engaged online. Often teens who regularly use technology are able to discern what type of interaction, language, and level of formality an online scenario calls for. In contrast, a teen that does not regularly interact with others online would certainly not be aware of online protocol or expectations of communication. Allowing youth to explore, ask questions, and experience a common technology scenario helps at-risk teens keep pace with their peers.

Technology programs also allow for mentorship and leadership opportunities among the teens. In another program facilitated by Czarnecki, youthful offenders were given the task of using Microsoft Publisher to create a CD cover to donate to a local homeless organization. The class was relatively unfamiliar with using Publisher, and so the experience had a learning curve. However, one teen in the class was familiar with Publisher and was able to use his knowledge to coach his fellow classmates on how to use the software. The result of the program was overwhelmingly positive. The teens learned how to use a new computer program, and also developed teamwork and cooperation skills. As teens grow into adults, skills such as collaborating and articulating their thoughts, both online and in person, are valued by employers and help young adults progress in their careers. Many of these skills, such as forming partnerships and working well with colleagues, can be difficult for teens to learn without hands-on experience. When properly facilitated, technology programs can make abstract concepts applicable to real-life scenarios and help teens develop important life skills.

Accessing the Internet

The Internet and its use are ever-present in modern life. Unfortunately, in many facilities where at-risk teens reside, particularly jails or prisons, the use of the Internet is prohibited. From a facility standpoint, just as hardcover books cannot be purchased because they can be used as a weapon, the Internet can be used to harm others and therefore must be restricted. Just as libraries restrict patron access to certain sites, youth facilities often have policies that prevent negative and illegal use of the Internet by the teens in their care. Facilities that house incarcerated teens or youth on probation are especially vigilant about Internet use, because they do not want to promote harmful or destructive behaviors among the youth. Although library staff must adhere to the rules of the facility, librarians can promote technology services to youth at risk by providing Internet supervision along with utilizing a wide range of educational tools to teach teens how to use the Internet properly.

One such example is a six-week workshop called the Edge Project that Czarnecki and library staff conducted in the spring of 2010 in partnership with youthful offenders at the county jail. The original project was a MacArthur Foundation–funded program and in partnership with Global Kids in New York City and a jail in Madison, Wisconsin. The workshop's primary purpose was for participating teens to use digital media to examine choices they have made that had a negative impact upon their lives, and to learn how to make different and better choices in the future. Participants explored a new online website each week, including VoiceThread (http://www.voicethread.com/), where they made learning maps and a time line of important events in their lives; Xtranormal (http://www.xtranormal.com/), where they produced a video; Bitstrips (http://www.bitstrips.com/), where they created an online comic strip; and GarageBand (http://www.apple.com/ilife/garageband/), where they composed their own music. Library staff supervised all programs and the teen participants learned new and constructive ways to utilize technology. Although it was important for the teens to enjoy the project, it was just as important for them to gain a deeper understanding of themselves and the consequences of their actions through the creativity of the programs. Librarians worked with teens to process the outcomes of the project and demonstrate the benefits of the digital media. This method also helped jail administration find the value of technology use, paving the way for future programs for the teens in their care.

Library staff should note that policies concerning technology use and the Internet are typically well established within facilities that house youth at risk. These policies can run the range from no Internet access for youth to access with supervision. As librarians form partnerships with youth-serving facilities, they must also familiarize themselves with their policies before trying to facilitate any Internet or computer-based program. Although librarians must adhere to facility policy, they are within their rights to find out the reasons for the policy. Librarians who work within a youth facility may find it easier to ask for an adjustment to the policy because they are employees and can facilitate programs on a consistent basis. Librarians who partner with a youth facility might have a more difficult time repealing Internet restrictions because they do not work at the facility full time.

In some cases, policies can be revised and access granted if librarians can make a compelling case for teen Internet use and demonstrate effective outcomes of a program. For example, the programs that Czarnecki facilitated with the youthful offenders had a clear lesson plan, with skills that the teens would learn as well as quantifiable results to show to facility administrators. When requesting a change in policy, library staff should write up a brief report for facility administrators that details the program, the equipment used, and how the teens will benefit from participation. Emphasize that Internet access will be limited to specific websites and provide a list of the sites targeted for teen use. If possible, having a product to show the administrators, such as a music clip from GarageBand, or demonstrating how Teen Second Life works can help facility management visualize the program and see the advantages for the use of the Internet. Librarians have a better chance of swaying Internet policy in their favor if they can present a focused approach to administrators. Instead of merely asking for the Internet to allow searches for content, present a proposal that specifies what teens will be looking for and how the Internet will assist in their search. Utilizing the local public library's catalogue for online subject searching is an excellent way to introduce teens to the concept of focused Internet use, and to show youth facilities how the Internet can be beneficial to teens.

If the request is approved, working with youth facility staff to formulate guidelines is the next important step in acquiring Internet access for the residents. Before engaging the teens in any online activity, library staff must be clear about the expectations and safety concerns of the facility. Although a facility may be comfortable with teens working on developing online communication skills, they may not be comfortable with the use of social networking sites or similar media, in which case the librarian would need to adjust the program. In addition, even facilities that already allow Internet access will most likely want librarians to identify program objectives and explain what kind of online activities will be available to the teens, in addition to the benefits of use.

In some cases, teens may be allowed Internet access as long as they are "supervised while online." This phrase might seem vague to librarians, and staff should again clarify the facility administration's expectations. For example, does "online supervision" mean that all teens explore the same website at the same time, or are they allowed to visit different sites? Are there Internet filters that restrict access, or are library staff responsible for filtering content? Is the setup of the library or computer lab conducive to supervision, or is it difficult for library staff to see what teens are looking at on their computer screens? If librarians are responsible for teen computer use, they should not hesitate to clarify expectations of the facilities and ask for support to ensure the success of their program.

Sometimes, despite the best efforts of librarians, administrators will not authorize a change in Internet policy for teen use. However, even if the fears of facility administrators are not justified and the policy isn't in the teens' best interest, library staff are not in a position to make changes, especially as a community partner. Ultimately, every librarian confronted with a permanent lack of Internet access must determine whether to accept the policy or move on to a facility that grants access.

Before objecting to facility policies prohibiting Internet access, be certain that giving Internet access to the facility's teens is relevant and can be utilized within a reasonable time frame by the teens. For example, librarians wanting to facilitate a program that teaches teens how to fill out online job applications should make sure that the teens will be released back into the community and are not serving long-time sentences. If the adolescents are serving twenty-year sentences, searching for jobs online is not the most useful skill for the teens to learn and not applicable to their circumstances. Taking into consideration the situations of the at-risk teens when planning activities seems obvious, yet it is important for librarians to remember to focus their proposals on activities that will benefit the teens in their present circumstances.

Czarnecki states that one of the most important tasks librarians must accomplish if they are allowed Internet use is to investigate the websites to determine if they are suitable for the program. For example, is a site blocked for some reason? Do any inappropriate ads appear? Is an e-mail account required? Does it take too long to load a video via a wireless connection? What images or sites come up when typing in a particular phrase? These are all issues to consider when deciding what websites will be accessed and should be resolved before the teens are in the classroom. Librarians should have a practice session with the websites before the teens are allowed to use them. If possible, ask facility staff to participate in a mock class. Evaluating websites with facility staff provides a second pair of eyes to catch something that might be missed, and also allows the staff to see what the teens will be learning and how it will benefit them. To ensure consistency with the equipment, Czarnecki also recommends checking all of the computers that the teens will utilize before the program starts because online information is not always displayed the same on individual computers.

A number of librarians may work in facilities somewhere in the middle of the spectrum, whereby only the librarian is given Internet access in the classroom and the students are not allowed on the web, even with supervision.

Czarnecki states that one way librarians can utilize limited Internet availability is to project websites onto pull-down or television screens in order to encourage group discussions. Staff can also allow one teen at a time to demonstrate a specific computer skill for their peers, such as uploading a photo or taking a screenshot. Even if providing the teens with their own computers is not a possibility, librarians should not feel that teens are not benefiting from the program. Great discussions can still happen and important skill sets can still be learned. In this scenario, librarians should view the program as an opportunity to invite facility staff to be present during class discussions that utilize the Internet. With staff involvement, it is possible for the facility to see that teens can use technology to improve their literacy skills, and this might lead to a more hands-on approach in the future. The sidebar on page 117 lists several online resources for keeping up-to-date with technology trends relevant to working with youth.

Beyond the Internet

When it comes to educating at-risk teens, use of the Internet can be controversial, but other options are available that do not require online access. One alternative is bringing library equipment such as laptops and wireless routers to youth facilities. Librarians should be aware that administrators most likely will want assurance that the materials are not a security risk to teens or to facility staff. In order to expedite permission, particularly when a considerable amount of equipment must be transported from libraries to facilities, librarians should photograph everything, including power cords, flash drives, disks, and controllers. They can then e-mail the pictures to their facility staff counterparts to acquire the needed approval. Often youth facilities require outside materials to be transported in clear containers or bags. Libraries can easily accommodate this requirement, although it may require the purchase of extra containers that meet facility guidelines.

Gaming is another excellent way to connect at-risk teens with technology resources. Video game systems are portable and do not require an Internet connection for use, although many systems have Internet capacity. Often facilities are hesitant to provide gaming programs to teens because video games are seen as extracurricular activities, not academic. However, research demonstrates that video games provide both educational and social benefits and can be used as a way to increase technology comfort levels, learning, and

Resources for Common Trends in Teen-Related Technology

- ALA Connect, http://connect.ala.org/
  This site gives members the ability to join groups or set up their own group around a collective interest, offering another way for librarians to tap into what their peers are doing regarding at-risk teens.

- PBS: *Digital Media: New Learners of the 21st Century*, http://www.pbs.org/programs/digital-media/
  This film, targeted at parents, teachers, and anyone concerned about education in America, explores how exceptional educators are increasingly using digital media and interactive practices to ignite their students' curiosity and ingenuity, help them become civically engaged, allow them to collaborate with peers worldwide, and empower them to direct their own learning.

- Internet@Schools, http://www.internetatschools.com/
  This journal is published five times a year and is dedicated to teaching educators about using technology and the Internet with youth.

- The John D. and Catherine T. MacArthur Foundation: Digital Media and Learning, http://www.macfound.org/site/c.lkLXJ8MQKrH/b.946881/k.B85/Domestic_Grantmaking__Digital_Media__Learning.htm
  As cited online, this site "aims to determine how digital media are changing the way young people learn, play, socialize and participate in civic life."

- Nielsen Ratings, http://www.nielsen.com/us
  Although not specific to teens, this site captures information related to what people watch and buy. Music, video games, television, and the Internet are some of the various technologies for which Nielsen provides information.

- Pew Internet and American Life Project: Teens, http://www.pewinternet.org/topics/Teens.aspx
  This site "provides information on the issues, attitudes and trends shaping America and the world."

- YALSA Electronic Discussion Lists, http://www.ala.org/yalsa/professionaltools/onlineresources/emaillists
  YALSA offers excellent electronic discussion lists and interest groups geared toward young adult librarians. These discussion lists provide a forum for librarians to discuss working with incarcerated youth and teens in juvenile halls, group homes, treatment centers, and mental institutions. Many librarians are using technology in a number of ways with similar populations, which makes exchanging information very helpful.

- YALSA Teen Tech Week wiki, http://wikis.ala.org/yalsa/index.php/Teen_Tech_Week
  This site provides planning resources for themed Teen Tech Week programs.

- YPulse, http://www.ypulse.com/
  This site studies current trends in teen media to provide information and news to media professionals.

literacy. Video games are a "cultural domain that requires interactive, evaluative knowledge" and can promote teens' literacy development just as much as a book club (Pierce, 2008: 59). The video games of today are highly complex, with many having their own vocabulary, storyline, and mythology. Participants are engaged in compelling ways and can become as emotionally invested as they would with a book or movie (Prensky, 2006). From an academic standpoint, there are a variety of educational video games that librarians can utilize to teach history, math concepts, science, art, and literature. Many games can be facilitated in a game-show mode, where multiple participants either play against one another or as a team to achieve the highest score. From a social standpoint, gaming promotes collaboration and team-building skills. For example, in some gaming scenarios, teen participants must work together to figure out answers to puzzles or questions. In other gaming scenarios, teens must take turns and share gaming equipment, such as controllers, and wait for their next turn to play the game. While these concepts may seem simple, they are fundamental to teen development. Respect toward fellow teens can be taught while playing video games by having youth encourage and support their teammates during game play. Patience can be taught and rewarded as teens wait for their next turn with the game. Teens are far more likely to learn and retain information if they are allowed a firsthand experience. While video games are fun, they also provide teens with challenges and learning experiences that are enhanced through technology.

Creating a video or photo story is another excellent way for libraries to provide technology services to teens. Videos and pictures enable participants to tell stories. At-risk teens who participate in such programs develop collaboration skills while working on different aspects of production that must be brought together to complete the project. Equipment for a video project can include Flip cameras, video cameras, or digital cameras that record video. Depending on the availability of equipment, teens can be assigned their own camera, or partner with another teen and take turns with the equipment. Teens can participate in tasks such as developing the story, capturing the footage, and editing the footage. These components can then be further broken down into activities that include sketching out the story, adding sound to the footage, or even serving as a mentor and teach other participants how to complete part of the project. Czarnecki recommends several excellent, free programs that are available for download and can be used for video-making programs:

- *Kodu* is "a new visual programming language made specifically for creating games. The programming environment runs on the Xbox, allowing rapid design iteration using only a game controller for input" (http:// research .microsoft.com/en-us/projects/kodu/).
- *GameMaker* is a program that uses drag-and-drop actions to create video games. Games can be made with backgrounds, animated graphics, music, sound effects, and even in 3-D (http://www.yoyogames.com/ make).
- *Scratch* is a programming language that makes it easy for teens to create their own interactive stories, animations, games, music, and art. Creations can be saved and shared on the Scratch website (http://scratch .mit.edu/).

Although having Internet access to enhance technology programs is preferable, it is not necessary in order for librarians to facilitate a successful program. The advantage of having a technology class where teens create a product, such as a video or photo story, is that librarians now have something tangible to show facility administration when questioned about the benefits of technology services for at-risk teens. When properly facilitated, technology can promote teens' growth and self-awareness just as easily as reading a book. Staff should not be frustrated if denied access to Internet use, but should look for other opportunities, such as the programs cited above, to promote technology use with teens.

Conclusion

Teaching technology skills to at-risk teens is an important part of librarians' jobs as educators. Because the definition of literacy has shifted to incorporate technology, teens need to understand how to use these skills in positive and collaborative ways. Although each library and facility is different regarding how much technology access they allow their teens, librarians need to find out where along the spectrum to start and move toward increasing access for at-risk teens. Technology programs can build teen self-awareness, promote creativity, and foster a desire for self-expression. Ultimately, these programs will help teens appreciate what they are learning and see the library as a resource for information technology as well as for books.

References

Braun, Linda W. 2007. *Teens, Technology, and Literacy; or, Why Bad Grammar Isn't Always Bad.* Westport, CT: Libraries Unlimited.

Eamon, Mary Keegan. 2004."Digital Divide in Computer Access and Use between Poor and Non-Poor Youth." *Journal of Sociology and Social Welfare* XXXI, no. 2: 91–112.

Lenhart, Amanda, Mary Madden, Aaron Smith, Kristen Purcell, Kathryn Zickuhr, and Lee Rainie. 2011. "How American Teens Navigate the New World of 'Digital Citizenship.'" Pew Internet and American Life Project. http://pewinternet.org/Reports/2011/Teens-and-social-media/Summary.aspx?view=all.

Nelson, Jennifer, and Keith Braafladt. 2012. *Technology and Literacy: 21st Century Library Programming for Children and Teens.* Chicago: American Library Association.

Pierce, Jennifer. 2008. *Sex, Brains, and Video Games: A Librarian's Guide to Teens in the Twenty-First Century.* Chicago: American Library Association.

Prensky, Marc. 2006. *"Don't Bother Me Mom—I'm Learning!": How Computer and Video Games Are Preparing Your Kids for 21st Century Success—and How You Can Help!* St. Paul, MN: Paragon House.

Rideout, Victoria J., Ulla G. Foehr, and Donald F. Roberts. 2010. *Generation M²: Media in the Lives of 8- to 18-Year-Olds. A Kaiser Family Foundation Study.* The Henry J. Kaiser Family Foundation. http://www.kff.org/entmedia/upload/8010.pdf.

Romero, Juan Suarez. 2010. "Library Programming with LEGO MIND STORMS, Scratch, and PicoCricket: Analysis of Best Practices for Public Libraries." *Computers in Libraries* 30, no. 1: 16–45.

Vahlberg, Vivian. 2010. *Fitting into Their Lives: A Survey of Three Studies about Youth Media Usage.* Newspaper Association of America Foundation. http://www.naafoundation.org/docs/Foundation/Research/Fitting_into_their_lives.pdf.

CHAPTER 8

Engaging At-Risk Teens

Teens enjoy and benefit from well-planned programs that are led by knowledgeable adults. Having programs designed for and focused on their developmental needs is especially beneficial for youth at risk. A well-planned library program for at-risk teens helps develop academic as well as social skills and can give these youth a sense of accomplishment. Programs that are well structured, are implemented with care, and provide participants with intensive exposure to a variety of program activities will have the greatest chance of benefiting high-risk youth. It is important for teens to develop positive relationships with staff, develop a sense of belonging, and have their needs and interests met (Public/Private Ventures, 2002: 11–14). Adolescents need stability and will thrive in supportive environments. Teens want to be accepted and respected. They also want to connect with the staff facilitating the program as well as their peers. Because of this, library staff can have a tremendous impact within the at-risk population. When we were interviewing library staff for this book, it became apparent that those who work with youth at risk are passionate about serving the population and genuinely care about the youth they serve. As demonstrated by the individuals interviewed, library staff who serve at-risk teens are resourceful, creative, and inventive, often doing much more with much less. They take the responsibility of serving at-risk teens to heart and consistently work to create programs that are both beneficial to the youth as well as fun.

Among the libraries surveyed, budgets and funding were consistently the biggest challenges staff encountered. Although several libraries were able to supplement funds for programming through grants specifically aimed at assisting youth at risk, many libraries struggled with reduced budgets. However, fiscal setbacks were not a deterrent and staff made do the best they could, utilizing library resources as well as items from home, making materials for programs themselves or asking for donations.

It became apparent that outreach is considered essential when serving at-risk teens because there are considerable barriers to serving these youth. The librarians we interviewed reported that the teens considered most at risk within their communities were not coming to the library. Transportation was cited as a major barrier. A library branch may have many outstanding programs for youth at risk, but if it is not near a bus route or within walking distance, if teens do not have money for bus fares or fuel costs, or if an adult cannot take them to the program, then the teens cannot come to the library. Another barrier was lack of comfort within the library. When teens considered at risk were asked by library staff why they were not visiting the library, the teens responded time and again that they did not feel welcome. A third barrier was awareness, in that the teens simply were not aware that the library existed. When facilitating outreach initiatives, library staff found many willing teen participants within their community who loved the library programs but, for various reasons, were not coming to the library. As a result, the libraries often took their services to the teens.

Community partnerships were also noted by staff as a critical component of serving youth at risk. Many library programs designed for youth at risk began with a partnership with a youth facility, such as a detention center or alternative school. Library staff found that these partnerships gave them a strong foothold within the at-risk community, allowing them to develop relationships with the teens and with the caregivers who serve the teens. Several libraries found that when teen participants were released from a partnered youth facility, they would become avid library users because of outreach programs they had participated in. Additionally, many teens who had previously shown little or no interest in reading became avid readers after they participated in library programs held at a youth facility.

Each library had unique examples of programs that worked with the teens of their community. The programs these libraries facilitated resulted in many best practices, which are shared in each Lessons Learned sidebar. In this chapter, the programs are organized into "Programs at the Library" and "Programs with a Partner Facility," yet the services can be modified to fit initiatives as needed. Forms referenced by library staff can be found in Appendix A. Librarians can use and adapt these forms and programs to meet the needs of their own teen populations. As libraries continue to evolve and work to include youth at risk, librarians are encouraged to use the programs cited in this text as a template and inspiration for their own services.

Engaging At-Risk Teens: Programs at the Library

Charlotte Mecklenburg Library, Charlotte, North Carolina
http://www.cmlibrary.org/

Librarian Tiffany Boeglen of Charlotte Mecklenburg Library wanted to create a "destination program" for the teens of the University City library branch (Tiffany Boeglen, e-mail/phone interview, March 2, 2012). The Charlotte Mecklenburg Library, which consists of 20 branches, had a strong teen summer volunteer program and Boeglen wanted to build on that initiative and offer teens volunteering opportunities year-round at her branch. There was a clear need for such a program because the teens that frequented the University City branch needed volunteer hours for many reasons, such as service requirements for school assignments or for college applications. A large segment of teens wanted a place to go when they were not in school so they could stay busy and "out of trouble."

Boeglen wanted to know what her library branch could do differently to accommodate more teens while ensuring that the library was still providing a relevant and effective experience for teen participants through the course of the summer and throughout the year. She asked branch staff for suggestions of duties that the teens could perform in each department, and also if there was a staff member who would be interested in helping develop a larger teen volunteer program. Larisa Martin, Library Services Specialist in the children's department, offered to help facilitate the program and also to find worthwhile projects for the teen volunteers (Larisa Martin, e-mail/phone interview, March 2, 2012). This partnership allowed the branch to take on more teen volunteers because there was more staff to help, and it also allowed the teens to have a broader volunteering experience that exposed them to more opportunities and growth.

Before Boeglen and Martin began the initiative, they first determined what the University City branch needed in terms of volunteer help. They created a needs assessment for the summer volunteer program and for the year-round program they wished to implement. The goal was to give participating teens activities that legitimately helped the branch and that the teens would find value in. They did not want to give the teens "busy work" or tasks that they would find boring. They collaborated with the circulation department and created ideas for teen volunteers that fell into four categories:

1. Ongoing responsibilities
2. One-time/individual projects
3. Downtime activities
4. Supervised ongoing/potential long-term projects

Boeglen and Martin then compiled a list of ideas for teen tasks, divided into the four categories they created. Examples of teen tasks included:

1. Ongoing responsibilities:
   - Hold and trace lists
   - Summer reading table
   - Assistance in programs
   - Weeding for condition
   - Computer sign-ups
   - Book displays
   - Reading buddies
   - Craft table
2. One-time/individual projects:
   - Carnivals/festivals
   - Summer reading displays
   - Individual Every Child Ready to Read/literacy-rich environment projects
   - Special programs (puppet shows)
3. Downtime activities:
   - Shelving
   - Craft and programming preparation (e.g., program setup or precutting of crafts)
   - Cutting paper crafts for bulk activities
   - Organizing material/craft packets
   - Craft planning
   - Cutting out shapes for summer reading
   - Book display creation and maintenance
   - Adopt-an-aisle (shelf-reading and fluffing)
   - Flannel/storyboard creation

- Weeding/weedlists
- Bookmarks
- Make old puzzle pieces into magnets
- Puzzle maintenance
- Reading buddies/spontaneous reading with young patrons
- Story sharing
- Cleaning mics/headphones once a week
4. Supervised ongoing/potential long-term projects
   - Storytime room cupboard inventory
   - Puppet inventory
   - Flannel inventory
   - Bulletin board maintenance
   - Making laminated craft "tables"
   - Possible puppet stage project
   - Thematic magnet board (updating magnets with themes)
   - Decorating projects
   - Flannel posts and pieces (kid-accessible flannel board)

Next they created a morning and afternoon schedule that had focused programs and duties based on the needs of the shift. Within the schedule, Boeglen and Martin determined how many teens were needed to complete the tasks. For example, a typical day in the summer could have the following schedule:

AM   Pull holds (1 volunteer, 1–2 hours)
       Summer reading table (2 volunteers, entire shift)
       Craft table/children's computers (1 volunteer, entire shift)
       Storytime (1 volunteer, 2–3 hours)
PM   Pull holds (1 volunteer, 1–2 hours)
       Summer reading table (2 volunteers, entire shift)
       Craft table/children's computers (1 volunteer, entire shift)
       Afternoon programs (1 volunteer, 2+ hours)

This method helped take a snapshot of what the branch needs were and where staff could use teen volunteers to fill them. After the assessment, Boeglin and Martin determined that the branch would need almost double the number of teen summer volunteers than in previous years. They were confident that their new method would work, and in the summer of 2011 they took on twenty-eight teen volunteers, where in previous years they had taken fifteen or fewer. The program was an immense success: teen participation skyrocketed and the University City branch had an extremely active and well-organized teen volunteer force.

Division of duties was important so that staff could stay organized and keep the volunteers effective. Boeglen was the lead staff for the program and the reference department contact. In this role, she reviewed volunteer applications and interviewed candidates, managed the master schedule of teen vacation/ time-off requests and any schedule adjustments, created a weekly volunteer schedule, and compiled a "Daily Duties" list for teens scheduled to work in the reference department. Martin was the contact for the children's department, where she compiled the Daily Duties list for teens scheduled to work in the children's department. She also reviewed applications and interviewed candidates and managed the largest number of teen summer volunteers on a daily basis. The circulation department also provided a contact staff member who compiled a Daily Duties list for teens scheduled to work in the circulation department and worked with teens on shelving and completing various reports. Boeglen created a binder that housed all information regarding the teen summer volunteering program. This binder, which was kept accessible to teens, had the sign-in sheet and listed Daily Duties clearly and concisely for each volunteer.

Interviewing teens was the next step and a critical piece in the teen volunteer process. The criteria for teen volunteers, whether they were applying for the summer or year-round program, required that they complete an application and undergo an interview (see Appendix A for example forms for a teen program application, interview questions, and skills assessment). Boeglen and Martin based acceptance to the program on the strength of the teen interview and the potential they saw in the teens. Not everything about the volunteers could be recognized on the application and interviewing became an important tool for staff to make smart choices regarding which teens were the best fit for the program. Boeglen and Martin tried to select the teens who would get the most from the program, while also contributing to the program.

"It makes sense to take the teens who are artistic, or the ones who are super bright, or the ones who need volunteer hours for school or college. But then there are those teens who don't really fit into those categories, and they don't have any volunteer experience. Maybe the library is their first experience in a work-like environment. During the interview is when you look for the teens who maybe have the untapped potential that the library can utilize," said Boeglen.

Boeglen stated that when managing a teen volunteer program, it does not make sense to take on a huge number of teens if the library cannot accommodate them or give them a positive and fulfilling experience. To cull through applications, Boeglen recommends offering spots to teens who do not have very much experience as opposed to teens who may already be volunteering with other organizations. "Sometimes we have to use that kind of information as an eliminating factor in order to give the teens who have not had the experience the opportunity," said Boeglen. She admitted it was hard to say "no" to the teens who did not make the program; however, the University City branch could not accommodate the number of teens who applied to the program. Boeglen stated that "no" is something teens will hear throughout their lives and is a part of growing up. However, if handled properly, "no" can be turned into a positive experience if the library is responsible and thoughtful about how the message is conveyed.

When the summer program concluded, Boeglen and Martin offered a scaled-down volunteering program during the school year. Teens had to apply and go through an interview process just as they did in the summer. Once accepted, they were required to commit to three consecutive months, which Boeglen called a volunteering block. She chose three months as the time limit because in "teen time," three months is a substantial amount of time. There are five blocks throughout the year:

1. September–November
2. November–January
3. January–March
4. March–May
5. Summer volunteer program

Within the volunteer block, teens must commit to a minimum of two to three hours per week at the library. Boeglen stated that she always prompts teens to start with two hours a week, which is the minimum, because teens tend to overestimate what they think they can handle. The staff usually scale the teens' time back and work to help volunteers set realistic expectations for themselves and budget their time. "Part of the job of volunteer coordinators is to recognize the strengths and weaknesses of teens, to take that into consideration when they pair teens together or when they are given certain tasks, and in addition to try to give them tasks that develop their weaknesses," said Boeglen.

During the year, Boeglen felt it was important to have an overlap month in the volunteer blocks to help with transitioning teens from one block to the next. For example, November is an overlap month, which allows staff to utilize teens who are currently active in the program and have them help train the new teens coming into the program. This developed teens' leadership skills and also gave them ownership within the program. Incoming teens also responded very well to being trained by their peers, and it gave them role models for volunteer behavior.

Participants were classified as either "active" or "graduated." Active teens were currently in the program and were supervised by staff, while graduated teens were previously active and were given more responsibility by staff, with less supervision. The program is structured to encourage strong volunteers to work toward graduated status. For example, if after three months teens do well in the program, they are offered another three-month block and can volunteer a full six months in the supervised yearly program. At the end of six months, if they are still doing well, they are then considered graduated and can participate in the "unsupervised" teen volunteer program. These teens have proven to be self-sufficient and dependable and are given a different set of duties than the active volunteers. The ultimate goal is to graduate the teens to the adult volunteer program when they turn eighteen and to retain them after they graduate from high school. Boeglen expects to have a fleet of well-trained adult volunteers who are deeply invested in their public library within the next few years.

At times, certain teens did not work out or did not follow through with their commitment. "This was where having a three-month commitment came in handy," explained Boeglen. After three months, the volunteers were reviewed and if they were not working out, Boeglen would have them take off a volunteer block and reapply again after three months if they were still interested. Boeglen stressed that it was important to keep the experience positive, to thank the teens for their service of three months, and to encourage them to apply again after a three-month break. Requiring the teens to reapply showed commitment to the program; it proved to staff that they were truly interested in contributing to the library.

As the teen volunteer coordinator for the University City branch, Boeglen experienced firsthand how the program benefitted the participants. One such teen, Miss D, was one of the earliest participants and for various reasons was easily considered at risk. Miss D, who was fifteen at the time, would often get in trouble at school or at home, and would talk to Boeglen about it when she came to the library. Boeglen decided to invite Miss D to participate in the summer volunteer program, knowing that she might require a bit more supervision. Miss D interviewed and was accepted, although she did not have any previous volunteer experience. Over the course of the summer, Boeglen said Miss D went through a transformation. She rose to the level of maturity and responsibility of her peer volunteers and excelled at the program. In the fall, Boeglen did not see very much of Miss D, until one day the girl visited the library and told Boeglen that her grades were improving, she was doing much better at school, and her home life was improving as well. Boeglen would never attempt to take credit for all the positive changes in Miss D's life, but she does credit Miss D's initial change in attitude to her time with the teen volunteer program. Miss D was not a traditional teen volunteer, but she was given an opportunity and she rose to the expectations that were set before her.

"Sometimes just believing in a kid can help them find a way to believe in themselves," said Boeglen. "If I can have a few more Miss Ds in my library career, I will feel like I really accomplished something. Sometimes the library can really make a difference."

Lessons Learned

As Boeglen and Martin developed their teen volunteer program, some natural best practices evolved. They found it beneficial to interview the teens in pairs because it gave two perspectives on the potential volunteer. They were also very open to taking on teens with less volunteer experience over those teens who had experience. They viewed the library as an opportunity for growth and designed the volunteer program to challenge teens, yet also set them up for a successful experience. Each teen volunteer was given a branch-specific orientation in which expectations were outlined from the first day of the program. The teens had their own volunteer handbook with their schedule and tasks outlined and easy to find. Boeglen and Martin held the teens accountable for being on time, having good attendance, and working to the best of their ability. They also communicated with branch staff and kept them aware of the teen volunteers. Through effective communication, they found more staff interested in supporting the teens with additional training, or suggesting interesting projects the teen volunteers could help with.

Boeglen and Martin stated the importance of getting to know the teen volunteers and not micromanaging the capable teens. They suggested recognizing individual strengths and weaknesses and pairing teens with complementary skills. Also, allow teens with experience to help train new teen volunteers when possible. This empowers the teens and also sets them up to handle more responsibility. Finally, let the teens know they matter. Hearing "good job" makes a big difference.

The Ocean County Library, New Jersey
http://www.theoceancountylibrary.org/

The Ocean County Library System has nineteen branches and two reading centers. It is a fairly large county system that serves a diverse population of teens. Within this population are factors that place the teens at risk for issues such as substance abuse, teen pregnancy, or gang activity. Through a generous grant provided by the Ocean County Youth Services Commission and sponsored by the collaborative efforts of many community partners, the library is able to hold multiple programs dedicated to the prevention of juvenile delinquency under the umbrella name of Tools for Teens. The purpose of the program is to raise awareness about the challenges adolescents face and demonstrate alternatives to these activities to the local teens, professionals, educators, and families within the community.

Supervising Librarian–Teen Services Coordinator Pham Condello, with the Ocean County Library System (Ocean County, NJ), believes that every teen will be at risk at some point in his or her life. "They will be faced with risky situations such as alcohol, drugs, or sex. Whether they will go down the road to actually being an 'at-risk' teen or not depends on their reactions to these situations," said Condello (Pham Condello, e-mail/phone interview, February 22, 2012). The ultimate mission of the Tools for Teens program is to provide resources for the teens so that they know how to cope with risky situations when they arise. Depending on the program, activities range from a lecture series to hands-on participation.

One of the most popular programs is the Gangwise Project, which educates parents and teens about the dangers of gang affiliation and offers resources to identify and avoid the gang lifestyle. This program is in partnership with local law officials and is presented by a juvenile gang expert. Some sessions are moderated by an ex–gang member or staff member who works in the correctional field. The library provides the space for the sessions, a projector, and a laptop. During the ninety-minute sessions, participants are educated about the warning signs of gang affiliation, the reasons teens join gangs, and information about gang identifiers such as colors, symbols, and clothing. Participants also learn about gangs in schools and within popular culture and are given advice on avoiding gangs. For one section of the series, the library separates the adults and teens into two separate meeting locations. The adults are educated about gang identifiers, how to tell if their child is in a gang, and actions to take if they suspect their child is involved with a gang. The teen session is usually facilitated by an ex–gang member or corrections staff member who discusses the realities of gang life and the consequences of the gang lifestyle.

"It's always satisfying to see a teen stay after to talk with the presenters on how they can personally escape the life of gangs. It's not easy when they can't leave the environment that they live in," said Condello.

Another highly popular program is the Support for Teen Parent series. This series is aimed at and focuses on teen parents and young adults who are new to parenting and provides information and resources for their children and families. Condello stated that each session has a very comfortable atmosphere with teens and their children in attendance. The four part series offers the following topics for teen parents:

- Session 1: Parenting and Finance 101
  This session offers an overview of parenting which includes: stress and time management, interpersonal relationships, dealing with special situations, and budgeting for new families and futures.
- Session 2: A Healthy You!
  This session shows participants that the best way to care for their child is to take care of themselves by making healthy choices. Representatives from the Ocean County Health Department speak about services they can offer. Local nutritionists provide information about healthy meals and speak about the importance of healthy eating for parents and their children. This session also discusses the importance of staying drug- and alcohol-free.
- Session 3: Teen Parenting Support Session
  Participants are given advice and support from experienced parents, including adults who were once teen parents themselves. Representatives from the Moms' Club of Ocean County also talk about the support they can give to the teens.
- Session 4: Playtime!
  Participants learn how to play and share stories with their babies in a way that will support a love of lifelong learning.

Other notable Tools for Teens topics have included:

- Man to Man—a mentoring program for young men that meets monthly to discuss issues that are happening within their community and ways to handle them

- Suicide prevention and depression in adolescents
- Drug use and abuse, including information about new designer drugs
- Bullying/cyberbullying
- Self-mutilation

One of the main challenges for any of the programs offered is transportation for the teens. The Ocean County Library System is part of a large county, making it difficult for teens to attend the programs. To combat this issue, the programs are usually held in at least three different branch locations within the county: one in the north, one central, and one in the south. Most of the Tools for Teens programs are located in one of branches; however, at times library staff have gone into the community to hold programs, for instance, if a branch location is too small to accommodate the number of participants.

Condello says that the programs are highly popular within the teen community, as well as beneficial. "One of our branches is in a community that is heavily populated by gangs. The Ocean County Probation Department court orders many of the juveniles who are in danger of falling into gang activity to attend our Gangwise Program. After these programs, many of the teens stay after to have one-on-one talks with the presenters about how they can get out of this way of life. One teen gang member, who I used to see during library time at the Juvenile Detention Center, left the gang lifestyle behind when he was released. This juvenile now speaks at select gang trainings and visits the library on a regular basis. The most recent time that he visited the library, he proudly came to seek a teen librarian to show off his poetry section in the high school newspaper," Condello recounted.

In addition to the in-branch programs, the Ocean County Library System created a Services for Incarcerated Youth workgroup that offers library services to the Ocean County Juvenile Detention Center twice a week, as well as to the Ocean Residential Center, a residential group home for at-risk teens. This workgroup meets quarterly to discuss the newest trends within this demographic, what services need to be added, and what needs to be altered. At the Juvenile Detention Center locations, library staff were able to develop ongoing services after receiving assistance through the Great Stories Club grant. Library staff were able to have extraordinary conversations about how these teens' lives paralleled the lives of characters in the books selected for discussions. The outreach initiative was so successful that the library is instituting a book discussion that will support the English class curriculum of the center.

Because of the positive impact libraries can have on the at-risk community, Condello maintains that the library needs to always strive to offer services to youth at risk: "We need to reach out to everyone and educate the community on issues that could affect their well-being. Many of these teens have no place to go for support or are unable to acquire the information or services that they need for a better life. The library is a place for all to get information and resources. They need to know that they can come here and that we can provide these services to them."

Lessons Learned

When determining whether there is a group of at-risk teens who need library services, librarians can look at community demographics to identify a potential target audience. It is also beneficial for library staff to be aware of what at-risk behaviors are happening within their community, such as gang activity or teen pregnancy, and establish whether a program is needed. If libraries are unsure of what is affecting teens, they can collaborate with fellow youth professionals, for example:

- School guidance counselors
- Local law enforcement
- Hospitals
- Health departments
- Municipal alliances
- Social services
- Local businesses
- Substance abuse counselors/groups

Condello stated that the Ocean County Library System begins planning programs six months in advance. "This gives us time to reach out to the partners and the communities to brainstorm ideas for our future programs. Once we come up with appropriate topics, we search for speakers and get the program details ironed out," she said.

When the program is organized with relevant content and presenters, Condello recommends sending promotional materials to library contacts, partners, community organizations, and the general public. The Ocean County Library sends hard copies of flyers and posters to partner organizations and e-mail announcements to a past attendee distribution list. Posters and flyers are visible and available to customers who come into the branches and may also be sent to outside organizations for display. The public relations department sends out press releases to all newspapers and local radio stations, and programs are also displayed on the library's website, where online registration is available and included in the library's monthly

(Continued)

Lessons Learned *(Continued)*

programming brochure. Condello stated that successful partnerships are an integral part of this process and it is important to make sure that all partners and cosponsors are acknowledged in any publicity. At the end of the program, it is important to thank everyone involved in helping with a successful presentation. And, on the day of the program, libraries may want to serve light refreshments because many of the attendees are coming straight from work or school, or may have their children in attendance.

Staff training is also paramount when creating initiatives that serve youth at risk, especially for the branch staff who may not have regular contact with this particular demographic. "I can't stress enough the importance of proper customer service to teens," says Condello. "Our library has ongoing customer service training for our staff."

Within library branches, staff should have a handout readily available that lists all local services that at-risk teens would potentially need. A prepared handout eliminates the need for staff to look up the information when asked, which can dissuade teens from seeking help. Condello noted that when a teen is asking for help, whether it be about homeless shelters or a suicide prevention number, staff does not want to take more time than the teens are willing to give. It takes courage for a teen to ask for help and the library must be prepared to direct teens to the proper agency if asked. To better assist teens, libraries may want to create premade handouts that list all necessary local and national agencies and their contact information.

Engaging At-Risk Teens: Programs with a Partner Facility

San Diego County Library/San Diego Public Library, San Diego, California
http://sdcl.org/
http://www.sandiego.gov/public-library/

Anna Hartman, Children's Librarian with the San Diego County Library– LaMesa Branch, and Youth Librarian Kirby McCurtis, formerly of the San Diego Public Library and now with the Multnomah County Library, teamed up to bring teenage parents the Cuddle Up and Read program, a storytime for teen parents and pregnant teens (Anna Hartman, e-mail/phone interview, March 6, 2012; Kirby McCurtis, e-mail/phone interview, March 10, 2012). The project was initially funded due in large part to an LSTA (Library Services and Technology Act) grant through a California Leadership Program called Eureka! Leadership Institute. The Cuddle Up and Read program is designed to empower teen parents to give their children the tools for reading and life-long success through storytimes and development of early literacy skills.

Pregnant and parenting teens are a unique user group for libraries, especially from a youth services standpoint because it is difficult for the teens to attend library programming with their children. Originally Hartman and McCurtis wanted to host special storytimes for teen parents and their children at their library branches. However, they quickly discovered the teens could not attend the program because they were in school during the day, or did not have transportation to evening programs. Hartman also recounted that several teen mothers had told her they would not want to go to a "regular" storytime at the library because they felt the adult mothers would judge them for being teen parents.

To find the right teen audience for their program, Hartman and McCurtis approached and partnered with four alternative high schools in the San Diego area that provided child care to their teen parents at the school. With this group of teens, Hartman and McCurtis were able to provide library services to teen parents, to their children, and to the teachers who work with the teens. Participants, both male and female, were teens who had at least one child, or who were expecting a child. The ages of the teens ranged from eleven to nineteen years old. The message of Cuddle Up and Read was the importance of reading to children every day and how to develop good reading habits at an early age. It was a message that Hartman and McCurtis wanted both the children and their teen parents to hear because reading is fundamental at any age. "Storytime is one type of intervention libraries can provide," says McCurtis.

Hartman and McCurtis visited school sites weekly with storytimes typically twenty to twenty-five minutes in length. They used a baby lap-sit model and incorporated the children into the storytime with their parents. They focused on activities the teen parents could do at home with their children, such as reading, reciting rhymes, singing, and playing. During the program, parents had a copy of the books read so they could follow along and explore the book with their child. Rhyme posters for each rhyme used or sang were created and enlarged for the group. The program utilized four storytime kits, which contained enough board books so all participants in the group could follow along, and included props such as finger puppets, shaky eggs, or scarves. Each family took home one bag filled with tools to help continue the learning. Inside each bag were five board books, early literacy handouts, and rhyme and activity cards. The cards had the rhymes learned in storytime on one side and activities to help work on early literacy skills on the other side.

The project goal was not only to teach the teens how read to their children, but to make reading, singing, and rhyming with their child part of their daily routine. This presented some initial challenges because the majority of the teens had never gone to a library storytime before and were a little reluctant to try it. However, there were teen parents in the classes who had attended a storytime and were eager to participate with their children. This encouraged other teens to try it, and once they did, they enjoyed the program.

Another challenge involved the teens' school issues. Although not all teens were poor students academically, they did have difficulties with school success, hence their enrollment at an alternative school. Some of other school issues included lack of discipline, language barriers, and poor attendance. Hartman and McCurtis explained that this made it extremely difficult to conduct pre- and postevaluations, and so they collected very few completed evaluations of the teen participants. However, they did hear about excellent results of the programs from the teachers of the teens and the day care workers of their children. "We got a report that the teens were reading more, and enjoying reading more to their children. They also were using the library more," said Hartman.

The program also had an additional benefit they had not anticipated: the children of the teen parents would ask to be read to and in their free time at the day care center were choosing to read a book rather than play with a toy. "During the conceptualization of the program the focus had been changing the focus of the behavior of the teens and not so much the children, and so this was an added surprise that the children changed their behavior as well," said Hartman. "I always told the teens that they were already reading for homework, so even if they are reading out loud from their textbook to their child, their children are seeing their parents read and that prepared them for (wanting to) read books when they get older."

McCurtis agreed and added, "It was important to remember and stress that for some of these teens, the at-home network of support was not necessarily there, especially for my teens who were living in a group home situation. Every opportunity for a teachable moment had to be seized and made relevant in order for it to stick with the teens."

> ### Lessons Learned
>
> School schedules often prohibit teen parents from attending a traditional library storytime, so it is important to make a partnership with schools and facilities that serve this population. Outreach to this population is vital because teen pregnancy has a negative impact for teens, their children, and the public sector. "Libraries have to see beyond the building walls and staff has to get out into the community," says McCurtis.
>
> Consistency is critical. The teens and their children need to be able to trust staff and will only do that after a staff member has been facilitating a program for a while. Hartman and McCurtis encourage getting creative with the traditional early literacy messages and adapting the model so that it is relevant to the teens' lives. Praise the teens when they are doing well, and give them respect because they are both growing up and raising a child.

Vernon Area Public Library, Lincolnshire, Illinois
http://www.vapld.info

The Vernon Area Public Library is a stand-alone library district and has a district population of 41,000 patrons. The library participates in a system that includes libraries across the Chicagoland area. The Vernon Area Public Library has an ongoing partnership with the Minard E. Hulse Juvenile Detention Center, in particular with the Family and Community Engaged in Treatment or FACE-IT teen residents. Within FACE-IT, residents are generally fourteen to seventeen years old but may be as young as twelve.

In the summer of 2006, Oprah's Angel Network awarded a Great Stories grant to the Vernon Area Public Library. This grant allowed the library to develop a new partnership with the 19th Judicial Circuit's FACE-IT residential treatment program, the result of which incorporated FACE-IT residents as members of the Great Stories Club. The project was highly successful with the teen residents and the coordinators decided that it needed to continue. The library and FACE-IT proposed the creation of the Read for Life program, which is a community partnership between the library and the juvenile detention center that provides books and programming to teen residents.

Gina Sheade, Adult Services Librarian with the Vernon Area Public Library (Lincolnshire, IL) and the Minard E. Hulse Juvenile Detention Center, is one of the facilitators of the Read for Life program. "Our program exposes at-risk teens to literature and authors they may not be familiar with and provides an opportunity to discuss books and other literature in a relaxed, nonjudgmental setting. It also enables at-risk teens to become familiar with libraries and library services," Sheade explained (Gina Sheade, e-mail interview, April 20, 2011).

Initially the program followed the guidelines of the Great Stories Club Grant, which helped implement the project and fund materials for the program. At the grant's conclusion, the library expanded upon and adapted the guidelines to establish new activities for the teens. Read for Life is still a monthly book discussion program held at the facility library, yet it also incorporates new programs, such as gaming and art. Books are central to the program and are provided to residents for discussions and to add to their personal library. For residents who have lower reading levels, audiobooks are provided to go along with the books selected for discussion in an attempt to increase participation. All residents, regardless of reading level, are involved.

In the monthly program, Sheade states that snacks are served and participants may select library books to check out following the discussion. Participants may keep their copy of the monthly discussion book. As of 2011, over sixty discussions had been held. When possible, the program invites authors to visit the group and participate in the Read for Life discussions. The short story discussion component of the program is a new addition and held every two weeks at the detention center. For this program, two short stories are discussed each session with three separate groups of residents. The library has purchased ten sets of short story anthologies, which remain at the facility for the program.

In addition to the monthly book discussion program, FACE-IT residents come to the library once per month for a two-hour Wii gaming session and snacks. There is also a weekly art program for FACE-IT residents at the Detention Center that is facilitated by a Vernon Area Library youth librarian. "The ultimate goal is to provide opportunities for at-risk teens to discuss books and other literature relevant to the challenges in their lives, and to encourage a love of reading and books and support of libraries among at-risk teens," says Sheade.

Since its inception, the program has yielded many positive results. Detention center staff have noted increased interest and enthusiasm among participants for books and reading. Many participants who previously had no interest in reading now look forward to selecting books at the library or reading the books brought into the detention center. Some participants also express interest in writing and sharing their writing with others as a result of this program. The FACE-IT teacher in particular has observed that the discussion component of the Read for Life program has enhanced the teens' understanding of the concept of "empathy," a key component of their treatment and rehabilitation. The teacher incorporates reading and preparation for the monthly book discussions into his daily curriculum and believes it is the most important thing the teens do. The success of this program has created a positive ripple effect in the community. Several community groups and organizations have come forward over the last few years to donate funds and materials to the detention center for various projects, and in support of Read for Life.

Lessons Learned

In developing a program to serve youth at risk, Sheade recommends engaging community partners. Once a partnership is made, library staff will need to identify a contact person such as an administrator, teacher, counselor, or supervisor who can give staff a sense of the "players" and the facility "politics." It is crucial to ensure that the facility director is on board with the intentions of the library. Give the partner organization a clear and simple proposal describing the proposed program and activities. Work with the library contact to create a program plan that incorporates institutional policies and procedures. A resource guide developed by the Great Stories Club project includes a helpful Sample Project Proposal Form (http://publicprograms.ala.org/orc/pdfs/GSCguide2.pdf).

Sheade explained that library staff maintains the library collections in the detention center, which includes the FACE-IT media center, the informal library space, and two collections in the detention area of the facility. This helped with knowing what materials were available for programs, and what residents were interested in reading. In developing activities for the teens, reviewing and choosing monthly discussion books and appropriate short story anthologies are ongoing activities. For each session, librarians prepare discussion questions as well as background material on the author, setting, historical context, and other relevant topics. Staff will bring read-alike material in case a teen's interest is sparked by a certain title.

"We hope the teens we work with in this program will develop a love of reading and enjoyment of books that will continue into their adult lives," said Sheade. "Also, by demonstrating what the library can offer and how librarians can assist, we hope at-risk teens will recognize the value of libraries in helping them achieve their educational goals now and in the future."

Loma Alta School/Marin County Juvenile Hall, Mill Valley, California
http://mcoeweb.marin.k12.ca.us/ae/lomaalta.htm

Creative writing instructor and Young Adult Librarian Katie MacBride volunteers her time and expertise and facilitates a weekly writing class for the incarcerated students at the Loma Alta School/Marin County Juvenile Hall (Katie MacBride, e-mail interview, April 18, 2011). The purpose of the class is to offer incarcerated youth an emotional outlet through writing and discussing literature and to help teens develop a passion for reading and writing. MacBride stepped in as leader of the class because there was not a creative writing program in place within the existing curriculum of the Marin County Juvenile Hall. In addition to facilitating the class, she brings library books that students request from the library in Marin County where she is employed.

MacBride states that the youth in juvenile hall have some prior offenses and may be incarcerated for gang-related activities, violent acts, theft, or substance abuse–related offenses. The facility is co-ed, but the female population consists of fewer than 15 percent at any given time. The majority of students claim that they don't read "on the outside," yet they are extremely avid readers when they are in the hall.

The writing workshop is an hour and forty-five minutes per week, broken up into two sections. MacBride begins the class with an icebreaker writing exercise. The class reads a short piece of fiction writing, and MacBride gives the teens a writing prompt based on what was read. At the end of the lesson, youth can choose new books to check out from a selection brought by Mac-Bride, and she collects books that are due and takes requests for new books. The supplies needed are minimal, such as paper and pens for the students. Most of the short stories used in the class are from the library, yet MacBride has also personally bought teaching aides and writing workbooks to help with lesson plans.

MacBride allows as much flexibility as possible in the writing prompt. The students can interpret it or change it however they want, provided it abides by classroom rules. If a student is having difficulty with the given prompt, Mac-Bride will talk through it with the student and help him or her develop an alternative prompt. To prepare for the class, MacBride is constantly reading short fiction, hoping to find short pieces of prose that will engage the students. She has found that the more engaging the students find the piece, the more receptive they are to the writing prompt and the idea of creative writing.

In addition to the books they request, she also brings a variety of books she feels the students might be interested in reading. If a student requests a book that is not allowed in the hall, MacBride suggests alternative titles with similar themes that are appropriate to the facility. She states that this goes far in maintaining a good relationship with the facility and the teen participants.

Although these might seem like standard library services practices, MacBride states that in juvenile hall, they are likely to be considered extreme kindnesses. The mission of her program is to engage teens with literature, and to encourage them to explore their creative potential.

"It is also wonderful to see improvement in students' work when initially they refused to write something. In general, just developing relationships with these kids and trying to convey that what they have to say is important."

Lessons Learned

MacBride states that it is essential for libraries to constantly assess the needs of the teen community and try to fill the potential gaps in service. Libraries that can establish a program or class as part of the curriculum of a facility will better meet the needs of the population. MacBride faced many challenges in serving the teens of the juvenile facility, such as language barriers, constant interruptions with phone calls, students being paged to various offices, and the ever-rotating population. As the population changed from week to week, MacBride initially found it difficult to create lesson plans for a stand-alone class. She discovered that flash fiction, or fiction stories that are 500 words or less, was useful because it is self-contained writing that is short enough to hold students' attention throughout the whole story.

MacBride found it was best for her to be the contact person to handle the library requests from the teens. She created an account for the juvenile hall so that she could check out and bring books to the students. Although she is financially responsible for the materials borrowed, MacBride states that getting the books to the teens is an essential part of her program, and currently there is not another option.

She reiterated that it was important to not assume anything about the teens in an at-risk program, because the teens have more to offer than what is detailed in their files or arrest records. "Get to know the teens as people and don't be afraid to share your own struggles. One can be personal and professional at the same time," MacBride states.

Library System of Lancaster County, Lancaster, Pennsylvania
http://www.lancasterlibraries.org/

Laura E. Kauffman is a Special Services staff member with the Library System of Lancaster County. Within this role, she is the sole facilitator of the What's Up with the Library? program at the Lancaster County Youth Intervention Center (Laura E. Kauffman, e-mail interview, February 16, 2011). The purpose of the program is to support and encourage literacy among the youth at the Lancaster County Youth Intervention Center and to lead them into a pattern of lifelong learning through reading, writing, and the enjoyment of their local public library. Participants range from thirteen to eighteen years of age. Kauffman states that the youth are often repeat offenders who have been in and out of institutions for much of their teenage years. Sometimes they are runaways, drug users or dealers, or teens who have struggled with violence. Consequently, the teens are mainly interested in books about situations similar to their own, such as living on the streets, being locked up, and overcoming addiction. Kauffman feels that What's Up with the Library? prepares the teens for independent lifelong learning by encouraging them to have fun while they learn. "I follow the philosophy that if they enjoy learning and succeed in learning, they will develop a desire to learn more," Kauffman says.

Kauffman visits the Youth Intervention Center twice a month for programs. The students learn about the libraries in Lancaster County and what the library has to offer that is relevant to teens. The programs are promoted within the Youth Intervention Center via handouts and posters. Supplies for the program consist of a variety of library materials and personal items Kauffman brings. Books, bookmarks, and library brochures from the surrounding counties are provided by the library. Kauffman also includes games and snacks that—depending on the budget—she either makes or buys. She has an extensive array of activities for the teens, including the following:

- Icebreakers—These are games that allow students to get to know the librarian and one another. Examples: group juggling, Two Truths and a Lie, Crumple, name games.
- Read-alouds—A book or part of a book is read aloud together as a group. The book follows the theme of the program.
- Movement games—These are games that allow students to learn something while getting up and moving around a little. This helps students overcome common stereotypes that the library is a place they must be quiet, or that there are not interesting materials for teens.
- Multicultural games—Students play Ampe, a game similar to "Rock, Paper, Scissors" that is played by school-aged children in Ghana; Mancala, a board game from Africa; the Native American game Stick, played by the Spokane Indians; and Civil War Slang, a matching game of slang phrases/words and their definitions from the Civil War era.

- Crafts—Students create art projects that relate to the theme of the program. Examples: clay beads, torn-collage journals, origami, marbling paper, tissue paper flowers.
- Library awareness—This is a description or discussion of the local public libraries and their services and a time for students to ask questions.
- Trivia games or contests—Sometimes this activity is a handout and sometimes the activity is facilitated as a game show. Students earn a prize if they win, such as T-shirts, candy, notebooks, drawstring backpacks, pencils, and so forth.
- Discussion—This activity can take the form of a book talk; other times it is a discussion about an event or book participants are reading.
- Author visits—The library sometimes hosts visits from authors to discuss their books and the writing process with the students.
- Demonstrations/workshops—The library will host magicians, musicians, jugglers, or motivational speakers.
- Summer reading—This is based on the traditional library summer reading program. Teens receive a form where they track the number of hours read to earn prize coupons to local businesses such as the bowling alley, laser tag, or restaurants.
- *What's Up? Magazine*—This is an in-house publication of the students' writing and artwork. It comes out four times a year and is distributed to all students residing in the Lancaster County Youth Intervention Center at the time of release. The covers are designed by a local graphic artist who volunteers his time and service to the library. When each issue is published, all residents at the Youth Intervention Center receive a copy to read.

At the end of each program, teens fill out an anonymous evaluation that helps staff understand what changes could be made to the program, what new ideas the students have, and what kinds of books should be purchased for their library. A similar document is given to the Youth Intervention Center staff to fill out as well. Through the evaluations, the programs have been proven to reduce summer learning loss, expose reluctant or struggling readers to engaging materials, promote critical thinking, and increase self-esteem and self-worth by providing opportunities to succeed. Kauffman maintains a data spreadsheet with all responses that she frequently reviews, and uses the feedback to alter and expand her programs.

All activities relate to a theme selected for a library program. Ideas may be found online, through other libraries, in the Summer Reading Manual, or in a book. After deciding on a theme, a program guide is created to record what materials were used and outline the program. Kauffman saves all of her program guides and rotates them to provide fresh activities for the teens. For each program, she also creates a booklist that is submitted to the center's program coordinator in order to purchase titles. Kauffman can also purchase some books from her own special services library budget, although her purchasing power is limited. The books selected for the teens are a combination of titles she believes students will enjoy, as well as titles they have asked for. For various reasons, the Youth Intervention Center library does not have a circulation system, resulting in Kauffman processing and labeling the books that go into the Youth Intervention Center library. Before shelving the books, she also enters the titles into LibraryThing, an online book-cataloging tool, so staff have a running list of what books are in the institution's collection.

To gain funding for her program, Kauffman often visits the county commissioners and keeps them informed of new initiatives at the Youth Intervention Center. As a result of this contact, the county commissioners provide some of the funding for the programs. Funding is a challenge Kauffman consistently faces. The library utilizes a portion of the special services funds for programming and book purchases at the center. Grants have allowed for the purchase of more books and incentives to give to the teens than the library would have been able to afford on its own. Although the program is valued, there is almost no budget for it. This requires Kauffman to be creative, making things from scratch and printing materials in-house for programs and activities.

Kauffman maintains that the program is worth the effort because it has yielded excellent results within the at-risk community. She consistently receives positive reviews from many teens both verbally and in writing through the evaluation forms for her programs. The teens respond well to the welcoming environment of the library, the engaging activities, the distraction of reading, and Kauffman herself.

"I have received letters from students upon their exit from the Youth Intervention Center. They share stories of hardship and struggle as well as stories of overcoming addiction and perseverance. They thank me for my program, tell me how much they enjoyed it, and how it has affected them. I find these stories very inspiring and they encourage me to continue what I'm doing," says Kauffman. "I go into my programs with an assumption that these students are no different from other teens. I treat them just like I would treat any other teen. I think my respect for them causes them to respect and listen to me. Providing a judgment-free atmosphere and just loving on them will have a great impact on them and encourage them to learn more about the things I teach."

Lessons Learned

Kauffman has found that teens react best to open, nonjudgmental situations in which the group can relax and have fun together. Icebreakers help facilitate a friendly atmosphere. The teens come into library programming and they are a little skeptical about what the staff is doing. Having a fun, often silly, icebreaker lightens the mood, helps the teens realize it's okay to talk out loud and laugh, and helps them get to know one another better, thus establishing trust. If staff can establish that trust in the beginning, teens will be much more likely to listen and participate in activities.

If possible, give them food. Teens in juvenile detention centers or shelters may only have access to cafeteria-type foods. Bringing in cookies, candy, snacks, and so forth, can really help to lift their spirits and again, can help establish trust with the librarian. Prizes are a great motivator. Some teens might not be inclined to read ten hours a week, but being promised a prize for doing so will be just the motivation they need. Libraries can have contests such as reading bingo cards with books from the institution's library, summer reading programs where they log hours, and essay writing. Good prizes include coupons to places they can go when released, such as fast-food restaurants, and positive activities such as bowling, laser tag, and local baseball games. Other prizes include journaling supplies, books, and toys/gadgets such as beanbags or key chains. Remember safety restrictions or the teens will not get to have these things until they are released.

It is important to listen to the teens. If staff ask what books teens would like in the library, write down the titles and actually purchase them. If the teens give a recommendation for a program, create a program with that theme. "If you give these kids a voice, they will feel empowered and will enjoy programs and the library on a whole new level!" states Kauffman.

Give teens avenues to success. Creating a literary magazine to which teens from the YIC could submit their writing and drawings made the teens feel successful. This kind of self-esteem boost can help them realize they can succeed in many other areas of their lives.

Typically teens sit during school, they aren't allowed much physical contact, they sit in their housing units, and they don't have gym very often. Get the teens moving around. For example, use books with activities such as *Pink and Say*, in which the characters play a game from Ghana called Ampe. It's a jumping, clapping

(Continued)

Lessons Learned *(Continued)*

game that resembles Rock, Paper, Scissors. Incorporate movement into the programs and the teens will be more ready to engage and learn afterward.

When purchasing materials for the at-risk population, Kauffman recommends selecting titles to which the teens can relate. Whether the books are about teens living on the streets, dealing with their parents' divorce, getting out of prison, or overcoming addiction, the teens really seem to latch on to books that reflect the circumstances of their lives. However, it is important to choose books in which the characters make good decisions or make the wrong decisions and face the consequences. "Don't glorify the very actions and attitudes that counselors and officers are trying to help them turn away from," says Kauffman.

Finally, make sure the teens know that staff care about them through their actions. Taking time to listen and be engaged with them during the library activities will have a profound impact on how the teens relate to the program, to the staff, and to the library.

Lafayette Public Library, Lafayette, Louisiana
http://lafayettepubliclibrary.org/

Amy Wander, Youth Services Librarian for the Lafayette Public Library, offers library outreach services to the Juvenile Detention Center of Lafayette (Amy Wander, e-mail interview, August 23, 2010). The Juvenile Detention Center houses teens aged twelve to eighteen, and Wander states that her library programs are designed to "reach out and connect with teens at a moment when they are often most receptive as they are away from their peers and their normal environments." Wander explains that many of the teens in the detention center do not know about or access the variety of services and books that libraries have to offer. As such, the goal of the outreach program is to increase teen awareness of library resources and to encourage library use both in the facility and once they are released.

The monthly library activities consist primarily of a read-aloud program provided by Wander or library staff, but can also involve special activities, workshops, and author visits. The center usually houses approximately 20 students who are split between three classes. These classes are separated by educational ability and include mixed grade levels. Because of the limited selection of books offered by the detention center, Wander decided to expose the teens to as much new material as possible by offering the monthly read-alouds. By diversifying the range of subjects and characters in the books,

Wander has tried to let the students know that regardless of their backgrounds or interests, the library has books for them. The books are often donated or left as a long-term loan at the detention center's library, so interested teens can finish reading the books during class reading time. Many of the books are biographies of adults who have survived adversity and proven that they can successfully turn their lives around. Wander states that the teens respond well to these stories and also enjoy reading realistic fiction. "After finishing an excerpt from the novel *Dope Sick* by Walter Dean Myers, one teen anxiously put out her hand hoping to be the first one to finish reading the book," said Wander. The book, naturally, went to the enthusiastic teen.

As with most libraries, the budget is a constant issue. Yet Wander, her library, and facility staff have found ways to provide popular books to the teen readers. For example, the public library provided each classroom with a set of the Bluford High book series on long-term loan. Wander says that the books work very well for the teen population because the titles are popular and can be read within the short stay that many teens have at the detention center. The detention center was able to purchase Accelerated Reader (AR) tests for the books so that students could keep up with the school AR program while in the center. Facility staff are also extremely supportive of library programs. After one read-aloud, a teen wanted to read the rest of the book and Wander did not have a copy to leave with the student. A detention center staff person went out and personally purchased the book that same week and the student was able to finish the book before his time at the center was up.

Wander says that the library is able to bring special activities to the detention center a few times a year. Often the events are programs that are happening at the public library, and the library extends the event to the teens in the detention center. "Bringing library programs to the teens is a great way to open their world to the variety of services the public library has to offer and to encourage them to use the library in the future," Wander says. Some of the most successful programs have been these:

- Poetry workshops—The library has offered poetry writing workshops some years but has also had the teens perform read-alouds. A variety of poems from haikus to full-page poems are brought to the detention center for the teens to read. Teens are asked to pick one or more poems that they would like to read to the group. The teens practice their poems during class and then recite the poems at the end of the class.

"Some of the teens are great performers and they really get to shine during this exercise," says Wander. The poems come from a wide variety of poets and reading levels from Shel Silverstein to Nikki Giovanni. As with most programs, the library offers this exercise separately with each class because the teens seem more willing to open up in front of their usual classmates. These smaller and more comfortable class settings make a big difference in the success of the program.

- Short story programs—The library has had the opportunity to be a part of a national grant program to read and discuss short stories with the detention center teens. The short story format works well for this population. This project has been a great way to introduce the teens to a variety of authors and to provide story characters in modern environments with whom they might identify. The grant has also provided the library with funds that have enabled the purchase of more books for the detention center library.

- Art workshops—Although art projects require a little more planning time because the detention center has restrictions on what materials may be brought into its classrooms, Wander states that these have been very successful activities. A photo transfer workshop that incorporated photocopies of photographs and packing tape displayed many of the teens' creative abilities.

- Technology workshops—Through a partnership with a local tech nonprofit, the library offered GIMP freeware photo manipulation workshops jointly to teens at the public library and to those at the juvenile detention center. The nonprofit group was able to provide one laptop for each teen during the workshop, so everyone was able to participate regardless of computer ownership or background. The teens thrived on the individual attention they received in these workshops, and after the program, one of the presenters commented on how the teens at the detention center were his favorite group to work with that summer.

- Author visits—The library has arranged several author visits for the detention center teens, including both local and visiting authors. A young adult author from a New Orleans nonprofit organization that works with high school students to write their own stories recently spoke at the center. The author had been invited to speak at a public library event and was more than happy to speak at the detention center, too. The author's age and biographical writing spoke well to this population and offered them a great role model as inspiration.

"It is always enjoyable when the teens feel comfortable enough to share their feelings and show excitement toward the books they hear and read," says Wander.

Lessons Learned

Wander affirms that interactive programs help engage the teens and give them meaningful experiences within the library. All library programs are designed to give teens a chance to shine and be creative. Interactive programs, such as the poetry and short story workshops, are easy for staff to facilitate and give the teens a chance to show off their personalities and their talents in a positive way. Wander stated that the teens are always well behaved and respectful during programs, but getting them to share their feelings in class can be a challenge. Experience has shown that smaller groups work better. Whenever possible, the students are visited in their own classrooms and not in the larger main room. Another challenge is to always be aware of the detention center's policies and to remain flexible enough to adapt and to work within these policies. Because the library is a guest within the detention center, Wander adheres to all guidelines regarding what items she may bring to the center and what titles the center deems appropriate to read.

Alameda County Library, Juvenile Hall, San Leandro, California
http://juviewrite2read.aclibrary.org/

Founded in 1999, the Write to Read program brings the library's motto of "infinite possibilities" to life as it motivates young people to strengthen their reading skills and make meaningful connections to authors and books that positively influence the choices they make in their own lives. The library program is a partnership between the Alameda County Library, the Department of Probation, and the Alameda County Office of Education. For more than 11 years, librarian Amy Cheney with the Alameda County Library has facilitated library services to the youth of the Juvenile Hall (Amy Cheney, e-mail/phone interview, April 25, 2011).

African American and Latino teens are the primary youth incarcerated in the Alameda County Juvenile Justice Center. Typically there are 200 boys and fifty girls at any given time. The average stay is two weeks, but many youth are incarcerated for longer periods of time, often on and off from age twelve to eighteen. Cheney states that the youth typically come from a background of intergenerational urban poverty, live in the inner city, and grew up with either a grandparent or mother, or within the foster care system. Naturally, their circumstances shape their personal and reading interests. The reading level for the teens ranges from preschool to adult comprehension with an average reading level of fifth grade. "Most teens have said that they did not use their public or school libraries to check out books, but once incarcerated they read more than they ever have in their lives," says Cheney.

She has found that the most successful programs feature guest speakers that both the staff and teens can get excited about. For example, teens responded well to author and lawyer Cupcake Brown, who survived the foster care system, overcame drug addiction and gang affiliations, and graduated with a law degree from the University of San Francisco. Teens also favored Ishmael Beah, the first child soldier to write about his experiences in Sierra Leone, and Azim Khamisa, who lost his only son to a drive-by shooting and now visits the teen who killed his son.

"It was wonderful because during the programs, the teens, probation officers, teachers, and medical and janitorial staff all enjoyed the visits," said Cheney. "And it also gave the teens something positive to talk about to the adults who surround them." When the staff are united by programs, Cheney says that it is much easier to get facility buy-in and support of future library programs.

Cheney has found that her teen patrons respond very well to someone who is twenty-five to thirty years old, is a person of color, and utilizes multimedia to present his or her own critical analysis of rap, racism, popular culture, and so forth. She determined this "magic formula" for speakers by watching who the teens responded to in the most positive way. If library staff do not know what their teens want, Cheney says that they must make it a priority to find out. "This can be learned in a simple conversation with a patron," says Cheney. "Ask them who their favorite singer is, what games they play, what their interests are. Just listen. They'll tell you everything you need to know to run a good program."

Cheney works to incorporate a variety of programs covering a range of interests to engage the teens. She has found that author visits, particularly focusing on people of color who have overcome personal hardships, resonate with teens. The library has also had success with visits by civil rights leaders and historical figures, writing workshops, tutoring, and book clubs. Cheney constantly seeks partnerships with community programs that focus on helping youth to make connections to organizations on the outside. Examples include the following:

- Street Soldiers—MacArthur Genius Award–winner Joe Marshall offers classes and free college scholarships; over 150 gang-involved youth have graduated from their college of choice.
- Homies Empowerment—Jefferson Award–winner Cesar Cruz offers field trips and speakers to gang-impacted youth to learn their history.
- Trips to plays and speakers such as Desmond Tutu
- Victim offender education groups
- Violence and male responsibility programs by ex-offenders

Cheney has found that many teens who leave the juvenile hall report reading more on the outside after they have enjoyed books while inside. She attributes this to the strong rotation of quality programs and materials the teens have access to while incarcerated. In fact, her biggest challenge is keeping up with reader demand while the teens are in the facility. "There are teens who have read everything in their interest level and beyond, and they want more books to read. They are ready for the next in the series because they are reading the galley copy that hasn't been published yet," says Cheney. However, she agrees that, as a librarian, it is a challenge she will gladly take.

Lessons Learned

"It is critical to have a program or an author that is relatable to teens, to stretch them and to find the link and help the youth find the relevancy," says Cheney. Libraries should not shy away from small programs; sometimes programs are better facilitated in small groups. The important thing is the program's impact on the teens. Cheney suggests bringing in the best community programs and resources so that teens can connect with the programs when they are released.

Cheney was able to overcome challenges involving materials, such as issues with hardcover books. The facility administration felt that the books were a potential security issue, because they could be used as weapons. The solution was to arrange programs featuring inspiring guest speakers for which the books were only available in hardcover. Cheney started small, in one unit, where all youth received a copy of the book. The administration and staff saw the value of the speaker and of the youth having the book after the program, and as a result there have been no other incidents with hardcover books.

"Librarians must understand the institution that houses the teens and its history with books and reading," says Cheney. "Find the people within the facility who support reading and literacy, and collaborate with them."

Conclusion

Staff who wish to serve the at-risk population will find that there is a supportive network of libraries and staff who are passionate about serving youth at risk and sharing the knowledge they have gained during their programs. Connecting with libraries that currently serve youth at risk is an excellent way to start a new program, especially at a library system that has previously not focused on this population. It is important for staff to remember that successful programs do not have to be replicated exactly as they were originally facilitated and can certainly be modified to fit the needs of one's own library system. Knowing how comparable libraries are serving youth at risk is useful, yet creating a program that serves the teen population of one's own community is even more useful.

Reference

Public/Private Ventures, 2002. "Serving High-Risk Youth: Lessons from Research and Programming." Public/Private Ventures. http://www.hewlett.org/uploads/files/ServingHighRiskYouth.pdf.

CHAPTER 9

Evaluating the Impact

As libraries move forward with initiatives that target youth at risk, they must consider how to sustain a program and how to make a lasting and positive impact upon the teen population. Concerns about budget and funding are central to every library, be it a public library, academic library, or school media center. Even when the economy takes a turn for the better, funding for teen services—and by extension services for at-risk teens—can be passed over for other library initiatives. Regardless of the age group or how excellent a program is, services can always be discontinued due to lack of library staff and funds. Often, services for teens are the first to be cut because attendance in this age group can be smaller than in children's or family-based programs. Libraries, which are dependent on public funds, private donations, grants, and other external sources of money, now have to justify their mission as never before. As programs continually come under scrutiny, library staff must be prepared to defend and advocate for their services for the at-risk population. Evaluation is essential to justify funds, staff time, library involvement, and even the jobs of the youth librarians. Library staff can have a difficult time validating the allocation of these resources to programs that cater to at-risk teens. Therefore, libraries must measure impact as well as attendance, demonstrate community need, and show administrators the positive outcomes of programs dedicated to youth at risk.

Evaluation of Library Programs

One major component of any library program should always be the evaluation. Many libraries do not gather evaluation data to help justify programs because in the past it was not necessary to do so. However, consistent program evaluations can be the library's first line of defense against budget cuts to services for at-risk teens. Evaluations can supply evidence that a program is effective and can demonstrate to administrators the positive outcome of the allocation of library funds within the community. Assessment helps improve program efficiency, allowing participants to offer feedback that can be used for future initiatives, and can indicate areas in which the program can improve. The data gathered can create opportunities for libraries to share findings with other similar programs and agencies, thus expanding the scope, quality, and range of services for teens at risk. The data can also make a case for continued funding for library services and for attracting new funding sources. If executed properly, evaluations can provide tangible evidence of program success and impact upon participants, which in turn justifies future initiatives. Program evaluations are proving to be required more often by stakeholders. There are common concerns, however, about program evaluations among libraries. For example, program managers may believe that evaluations are an additional burden on library staff. Evaluations could potentially divert resources away from a program if they provide negative results. Some librarians might see evaluations as too complicated for staff and for patrons, or they might view them as just another form of program monitoring (Metz, 2007).

Although all of these concerns are valid, it is important for libraries to realize that the expectations of budget administrators and communities are changing. Libraries are still a viable and vital part of society, but now must validate budgets, staff time, services, and their place in the community. Libraries committed to serving youth at risk very likely will have to carefully document and substantiate programs offered if they wish to provide consistent service to teens. Staff time is, of course, valuable and will be impacted by the extra effort of evaluations. However, libraries can ease the burden of evaluations through planning, utilizing current information, and asking for assistance with surveys.

Libraries are already adept at collecting user statistics that help demonstrate patron use and interest, such as circulation numbers and program attendance. Library staff can easily gather patron statistics if a program called for them. If a library is partnered with a facility, the library can request assistance with evaluations. Many youth facilities have their own evaluation process, and libraries can save time and effort by asking their partners to share findings or include questions relevant to library services within surveys. If a library must create and administer evaluations from scratch, streamlining the surveys and gathering the data necessary to show program outcomes can help minimize the burden on staff. To ensure the evaluations will gather the information needed and that they make sense to adolescent readers, staff might consider having the questions reviewed by an independent evaluator before they are administered to the teens. An evaluation does not have to be complex to gather the information needed. Because staff may have limited time to administer the surveys, or the teens may have limited focus, librarians are advised to keep surveys simple and straightforward in order to gather the best results. For examples of evaluations using outcome-based measurements, refer to Appendix A of this text.

Because libraries must determine which programs work and which do not, monitoring programming through evaluations can help library administrators assess whether a program is in compliance with specified performance standards, such as the number of participants served, and if expected outcomes were achieved (Metz, 2007). It is just as important for libraries to gather information about programs as it is to ask the questions that best demonstrate the positive outcomes of services for teens. Libraries can also use "stories of impact" to highlight services to patrons that yield outstanding results. They are in essence a snapshot of a program or initiative and typically focus on one patron's experience with the library and the outcome of library service. Example stories of impact are detailed further in this chapter, and Appendix A includes a form that librarians can use to develop their own stories of impact.

Output Measures versus Measurable Outcomes

The way that a survey question is phrased or an evaluation is worded can make a difference in the information gleaned from participants. When gathering data and statistics, libraries most often rely on output measures to evaluate program success. Output measures are defined as counts of an activity, information that most libraries are exceptionally good at collecting (Matthews, 2010). The following are examples of output measures that encompass teens:

- Number of teens registered for the summer reading program
- Number of teens attending program events
- Number of teens completing a program
- Number of young adult materials checked out
- Number of literacy-based programs for teens
- Total attendance of participants at teen-related programs
- Number of new library cards issued to teens per year

Output measures are an excellent way to gather statistics for teen programs and to reflect the use of the library by the young adult population. By their design, libraries are already set up to collect data through output measures. Circulation statistics, library card applications, and program attendance can easily be tracked and utilized to demonstrate teen use. However, evaluations can be taken a step further by employing the use of measurable outcomes. Measurable outcomes, also referred to as outcome-based performance measures, attempt to measure the result programs have in the lives of the participants, their families, and the community in which they reside (Matthews, 2010). Outcomes help answer the question of *why* libraries provide services to patrons and if there is a benefit to the effort staff are putting into an initiative. An outcome asks, "What value does the library bring to the community?" and helps demonstrate that the resources and services provided are producing positive results (Boudreau, 2011). In order for an outcome-based measurement to resonate with decision makers, at least two of the following criteria should be met:

- The program and the outcome must be closely linked; there must be a cause-and-effect relationship. For example, "If this happens, then this will result."
- The outcome must be measurable in a consistent and reliable manner. (Matthews, 2010)

Using the outcome-based evaluation method helps to justify programs by telling "the library story" to administrators. The result of an outcome-based program combined with statistics from output measures can clearly demonstrate how budget money and staff time are being spent and show quantifiable results of teen participation in library programs. Library staff can utilize the data produced to demonstrate the impact of services on at-risk teens, which can justify the time and expense of programs to stakeholders. Outcomes reflecting participant progress, growth, and constructive behavior show positive results of library initiatives. Library outcomes can reflect how teens gain insight into the beliefs and values of others through programs such as book clubs, author visits, and literary discussions, or through having access to a diverse young adult collection. The at-risk population, which benefits greatly from library services, can provide incredible stories of impact and development that can help staff advocate for continual involvement with the population.

Creating and Using Measurable Outcomes with At-Risk Teens

In the past, libraries have traditionally used outputs as their sole evaluation tool. Library services and budgets could easily be justified by demonstrating how many patrons came to programs, checked out books, or walked through the front door. However, as the economy has become increasingly unstable, competition for library funding has increased. No longer can libraries use only door count or circulation statistics to validate annual budgets. Financial resources such as grants, endowments, and funding have become increasingly difficult to obtain. Libraries must now be prepared to defend programs and services to their stakeholders, particularly those that focus on at-risk teens. Utilizing measurable outcomes in conjunction with output measures, libraries can demonstrate to stakeholders and administrators what services the institution provides, and how those services impact at-risk teens. See the top sidebar for examples of me organization asurable goals and objectives for library programs geared toward at-risk teens.

Because libraries already gather and can readily produce output measures, the question might arise as to why libraries would want to use the measureable outcome

---

Examples of Measurable Goals and Objectives

- Increase accessibility of library resources to youth at risk by 25 percent in 2012, or seventy-five more teens than in 2011.
- Increase teen enrollment and attendance in library programs during the next twelve months by fifty participants or 15 percent more than the previous twelve-month period.
- Increase circulation of materials to youth at risk by 5,000 items annually, representing an overall increase of 25 percent more than last year.

Examples of How Success Can Be Measured

- The number of at-risk teen patrons served will increase by 15 percent during the twelve-month program period.
- Success will be measured if 30 percent of teen participants are able to utilize online resources for school work and completion of their Senior Exit project. Success will be assessed by an independent program evaluation performed by the community partner of the library program.
- At least 75 percent of participants in the Mom and Me storytime program will demonstrate at least eight of the twelve early literacy competencies with their child at the conclusion of the four-week workshop.

Example of Library Story of Impact

Person: Miss J was a teen mom who had never taken her one-year-old child to storytime, nor had ever attended one herself.

Problem: Miss J wanted to read to her daughter, but was not sure what books to pick out or what her daughter would like.

Library intervention: The teen librarian connected Miss J with the Mom and Me storytime program, a library outreach program facilitated at the City Recreation Center near her high school. The librarian also helped Miss J obtain a library card and took her to the children's department to help with book selection for her daughter.

Happy ending: Miss J and her daughter regularly attend the Mom and Me storytime, and she checks out books from the library each week. Miss J says she reads to her daughter almost every night. Miss J's daughter is now starting to recognize colors and shapes.

Final write-up: Miss J was a teen mom who had never taken her one-year-old child to storytime, nor had ever attended one herself. Miss J wanted to read to her daughter, but was not sure what books to pick out or what her daughter would like. The teen librarian connected Miss J with the Mom and Me storytime program, a library outreach program facilitated at the City Recreation Center near her high school. The librarian also helped Miss J get a library card and took her to the children's department to help with book selection for her daughter. Miss J and her daughter regularly attend the Mom and Me storytime, and she checks out books from the library each week. Miss J says she reads to her daughter almost every night. Miss J's daughter is now starting to recognize colors and shapes.

---

method, especially when it can be a time-consuming process. Perhaps the best rationale for utilizing outcome-based measurements is that it is a language that stakeholders and financial decision makers understand. When the economy suffers and access to funding becomes competitive, budgets for library programs can be reduced or taken away altogether. In some cases, the library is not included as an educational institution, even though students both in and out of school environments utilize its resources. Libraries need to be able to articulate what services they provide, how the services affect their patrons, and the value—both monetarily and to the community—of the services. They are, in essence, telling the story of how libraries impact their patrons. In this regard, there are many benefits to using outcomes in evaluating services. Outcome data can be used to do the following:

- Strengthen existing services
- Target effective services for expansion
- Identify staff and volunteer training needs
- Develop and justify budget
- Prepare long-range plans
- Focus decision makers' attention on programming needs and issues
- Demonstrate that inputs and activities are producing measurable results
- Determine if improvements need to be made, if the program should be done differently, or if there is even a need for the program (Boudreau, 2011)

In order to have the greatest success with outcome-based evaluation, it should be a part of the initial planning process, not something added on at the end of the program. Tacking it on at the end will not produce accurate results and will render the evaluations invalid. Programs that have the most success with outcome-based evaluations implement the method at the beginning of the program and see it all the way through to its conclusion.

One of the most difficult aspects of the process is identifying and articulating what the measurable outcomes should be and how to create the evaluation. Before a library begins to work with at-risk teens, it must ask how the program benefits the participants and ascertain how to measure the results. When crafting a program with outcome-based measurements, libraries can utilize the logic model conceptual chain to help develop results with maximum impact. The logic model conceptual chain is a visual depiction of related events that connects the need for a program with the desired outcome for the program (Boudreau, 2011). The logic model concept asks libraries to determine the following foundations for their potential programs:

- Need
- Goal
- Target population
- Theory
- Input
- Activities
- Output
- Outcome

Using this method, libraries can create outcome-based measurements that reflect the impact of their efforts within the at-risk community. Appendix A includes a form that librarians can use to develop an evaluation plan.

Need

Libraries must clearly state the need of the at-risk population. Although this sounds like an obvious step, it is important for the library to focus on a particular segment of the at-risk population. "At risk" denotes a large demographic of teens and to better display the impact of their services, libraries will need to narrow down who they wish to serve. For example: "Within Community X, only 40 percent of high school freshmen know how to successfully develop and write a research paper. Freshmen will need to know how to develop and write a research paper for the Senior Exit project."

In this case, the need is to *improve the research skills of high school freshmen within Community X*. Libraries can zero in on a population even further, but using identifiers such as community, school, and age range is an excellent place to start when stating the needs of a population. When the need is determined, libraries can utilize community sources, such as the Census Bureau, the Health Department, or school statistics to provide data to validate services. Because libraries define the need, it is important to determine what they are uniquely qualified to do to answer it. For example, perhaps there is an initiative already addressing this need within the at-risk community. If this is the case, the library might want to determine if it is appropriate to partner with the initiative and offer support, or move on to another segment of the at-risk population that is not getting support. Keep in mind that if another organization is assisting the at-risk population in conjunction with the library, it may be difficult for the library to demonstrate measurable outcomes that can be attributed solely to a library program. When determining the need for a program, libraries should consider whether they would be duplicating services that are already being provided to at-risk teens. This is not a wise use of resources, does not resonate with stakeholders, and does not ultimately help the teens. In determining need, libraries should choose an at-risk population for whom service can do the most good and make a lasting and positive impact.

Goal

Once the need has been determined, libraries can create the goal for their program. The goal is the desired outcome and what libraries are working toward as they facilitate their services to at-risk teens. The goal can be broadly stated but should clearly connect to the desired outcome. For example: "The library program will foster a love of reading in participants, improve reading comprehension and retention, improve students' research skills, etc." At this point in the planning process, the methods used to achieve the goal are not as important as the goal itself. The goal is the final product and where libraries hope their young patrons will be as a result of their services. The goal should be focused on the identified patron group, and most important, be something that libraries can feasibly accomplish. Appendix A includes a form that librarians can use in the process of goal development.

Target Population

For the target population, libraries are describing the at-risk teens that they desire to serve. Identifiers such as age group, gender, race, socioeconomic status, disability, and so forth, should be cited, along with unique characteristics of the population, and geographic location or the community/area of focus (Boudreau, 2011). For example: "The target population will be rising high school freshmen at the Example High School who do not readily have access to online databases or Internet resources, and are low-performing in their English composition class." The teens served can easily be a group within the population, such as a single class or after-school group of students. For the purposes of creating a measurable outcome, the target population does not have to be a large group and can be a sampling of the teens the library desires to work with. If an initiative is new, libraries may want to focus on a small and manageable group where measurables can be easily collected, and try reaching a larger population if the service is a success.

Theory

In this section, libraries will explain their theory as to why they chose to work with their target population, and why the program will be a success. A well-articulated theory will demonstrate the program's ultimate success with the target population by citing the following:

- Industry best practices
- Research-based service delivery strategies
- Replication of a model from another region (Boudreau, 2011)

For example:

- YALSA recommends the following techniques to engaging reluctant readers . . .
- Academic studies show that high school students who learn how to conduct research for high school papers are better prepared for college.
- These successful programs have been used by the Example Library System . . .

By citing best practices and research related to the theory, libraries can support their programs for at-risk teens.

Input

Input details the resources that libraries will need to successfully facilitate their programs. For example: "The library will need a budget of X dollars and X amount of staff. The library will also need access to current databases to facilitate the program." To further explain the input section, libraries can include a detailed budget, allocation of staff time, special skills that staff would need to facilitate the program, titles of books, lists of equipment, recommended reference materials, and so forth. The more detailed the input section, the clearer the picture will be of what is needed to serve youth at risk. It is even possible to make a case for more resources, and perhaps gain more support for the program in its initial development.

Activities

This section describes what will be done with the input to fulfill the program goal. What programs and services will be facilitated for the at-risk population? For example: "Freshmen students at Example High School will participate in a library-lead book club during the fall semester that will study graphic novels. At the conclusion, students will use the public library database and resources to write a one-page research paper about the graphic novel author or illustrator of their choice." Libraries can make this section as detailed as they feel is needed. Depending on the stakeholders, a lesson plan for each session and how it will be facilitated might be appropriate, or a summary might suffice. Libraries should use their judgment when completing this section, and use whichever course of action will garner the most support.

Output

Output is "the direct products of program strategies, activities, and/or events" (Boudreau, 2011). Outputs are circulation statistics, number of program attendees, reference stats, and so forth. For example: "During the course of the program, the library served X high school freshmen over X weeks, for a total of X sessions." Outputs are valuable as they measure the quantity of work done by participants, and whether the program was delivered the allotted number of times intended to participants. Libraries excel at measuring outputs, and will only need to refer to their stats to collect this valuable data.

Outcome

The outcome is the final section of the measurement and the most important. Outcomes are "specific statements of the benefits of changes experienced by individuals or groups during or after participation in the program" (Boudreau, 2011). Outcomes relate to the teens listed in the target population. They are a direct result of program activities and follow a logical progression in relation to the stated theory. For example: "If low-performing freshmen participate in the library outreach initiative, then the students will be able to successfully utilize the library catalog to research future projects. At the conclusion of the program, at least 60 percent of rising freshmen will be able to successfully utilize library databases to complete their research papers." Outcomes are always portrayed as constructive; they do not reflect what did not happen, but what *did* happen within the at-risk population. The library should ultimately be able to demonstrate that the outcome produced a positive development in the knowledge, attitude, behavior, skill, or condition of at-risk teens because of deliberate action on the part of library staff.

Measuring the Impact

The most important thing to keep in mind when developing the outcome is, is it measurable? Can the projected outcome be proven with test scores, grades, or student knowledge, or demonstrated in terms of participant performance? Can the library link a change in behavior or attitude within the at-risk population to a specific program? Within a logic model, there are typically three types of outcomes: initial, intermediate, and long term. An initial outcome is the benefit of a patron's experience, such as new knowledge or a new skill learned. The intermediate outcome is a change in a patron's behavior that results from this new knowledge or skill. The long-term outcome represents a meaningful change for participants that relates to their condition or status (Boudreau, 2011). When measuring the results of outcome-based programs, stakeholders typically want to see data that reflects an increase in skill, knowledge, or positive development within the target population.

Libraries can demonstrate these results by articulating the result of the outcome in terms of initial, intermediate, and long-term development. For example: "If low-performing freshmen participate in the library outreach initiative, then the students will be able to successfully utilize the library catalog to research future projects."

- The *initial outcome* of the targeted freshmen participating in the library outreach initiative will result in their ability to successfully utilize the library catalog and resources for school projects.
- The *intermediate outcome* of the targeted freshmen participating in the library outreach initiative will result in the students gaining newfound academic confidence.
- The *long-term outcome* of the targeted freshmen participating in the library outreach initiative will result in their development of an educational skill that will serve them throughout their high school experience, which increases their opportunity to attend college, and provides a foundation for college-level academic work.

Whichever method the library selects to demonstrate the outcome of a service or initiative, outcomes must be measurable in a consistent and reliable manner. Evaluations of this nature take time, effort, and planning on the part of the library. However, once an in-depth evaluation has been completed, libraries can build on best practices and use procedures for future programs.

Another method libraries can utilize to show the value of services to at-risk teens is to share stories of impact with stakeholders. A story of impact relates how the library has affected one patron in relation to a larger initiative. This method puts a face to the teens that use the service, allowing for a more personal connection. Jamie LaRue, Director of Douglas County Libraries, Colorado, shared a simple definition of a "story of impact" with North Carolina public library directors at an advocacy workshop in 2011. According to LaRue, a story of impact has four pieces:

1. Person
2. Problem
3. Library intervention
4. Happy ending (LaRue, 2011)

Example of Complete Logic Model Concept

1. **Need:** Within Community X, only 40 percent of high school freshmen know how to successfully develop and write a research paper. Freshmen will need to know how to develop and write a research paper for the Senior Exit project.

2. **Goal:** The library program will improve students' research skills and enable them to successfully develop and write a research paper. At the conclusion of the program, 75 percent of teen participants will be able to develop and create a research paper.

3. **Target population:** The target population will be rising high school freshmen at the Example High School who do not readily have access to online databases or Internet resources, and are low-performing in their English composition class. For this program, the library will partner with Mrs. Smith's English class, which has eighteen freshmen.

4. **Theory:** Academic studies show that high school students who learn how to conduct research for high school papers are better prepared for college. The Mid-Sized Library facilitated a similar research program in 2010 titled "Ready, Set, Research!" The Mid-Sized Library provided freshmen students training and access to their ERIC database during a six-week on-site program. At the beginning of the program, 25 percent of students could successfully research a topic for school. At the conclusion of the program, 60 percent of the students could successfully research a topic for school.

5. **Input:** The library will need two librarians who are well-versed in research methods and database use. The librarians will be using their branch laptops and flash drives to facilitate the program. The school will provide computers in the school computer lab for the program.

6. **Activities:** Eighteen freshmen in Mrs. Smith's English class will participate in a six-week program detailing how to use online databases to develop and write a research paper. Sessions will be held at the high school and will last one hour. The weekly breakdown is as follows:

Week One	Introduction to online databases: ERIC, WorldCat, and beyond.
Week Two	Finding the right information: Why Google and Wikipedia aren't always the answer.
Week Three	How to select a topic for a successful research paper.
Week Four	What information will you need to research?
Week Five	Researching your topic.
Week Six	Writing and citing your research.

7. **Output:** During the course of the program, the library served eighteen high school freshmen over six weeks, for a total of six sessions.

(Continued)

Example of Complete Logic Model Concept *(Continued)*

8. **Outcome:** At the conclusion of the program, 95 percent of teen participants could successfully develop a research paper. Mrs. Smith stated that sixteen of her eighteen students could use online databases to find reliable information that supported the topic of their research paper. The two who did not know how to utilize online databases had missed four of the six sessions. Additionally, after completion of the program, all eighteen participants saw an increase of at least one letter grade in their English class with Mrs. Smith in the following semester.

Story of Impact

- *Person*—Tommy was a freshman at Example High School. During the first semester of his freshmen year, he consistently made Cs or lower on his research papers for English class.
- *Problem*—Tommy would frequently get frustrated with writing research papers, because he did not know how to find reliable information, and did not know how to structure and cite his work. Although he knew he would be expected to select and research a topic for his Senior Exit project, he did not think he would be able to do so, and did not think he would graduate.
- *Library intervention*—Tommy participated in the six-week research program facilitated by the public library. Librarians showed Tommy how to select a topic for research, how to use online databases to find reliable information, and how to properly write and cite sources within a research paper.
- *Happy ending*—Tommy researched and wrote a paper after the conclusion of the six-week library program and earned an A on his paper. Tommy has consistently made B+ to A on all of his English research assignments. Most important, Tommy now feels that he can write his Senior Exit research paper, and that he will graduate in 2016.

Final Write-Up

Within Community X, only 40 percent of high school freshmen know how to successfully develop and write a research paper. Freshmen need to know how to develop and write a research paper for the Senior Exit project. The library program will improve students' research skills and enable them to successfully develop and write a research paper. At the conclusion of the program, 75 percent of teen participants will be able to develop and create a research paper. The target population will be rising high school freshmen at the Example High School who do not readily have access to online databases or Internet resources, and are low-performing in their English composition class. For this program, the library will partner with Mrs. Smith's English class, which has eighteen freshmen. At the conclusion of the program, 95 percent of teen participants could successfully develop a research paper.

(Continued)

Final Write-Up *(Continued)*

Mrs. Smith stated that sixteen of her eighteen students could use online databases to find reliable information that supported the topic of their research paper. The two who did not know how to utilize online databases had missed four of the six sessions. Additionally, after completion of the program, all eighteen participants saw an increase of at least one letter grade in their English class with Mrs. Smith in the following semester.

The program is best summed up with the success of Tommy. Tommy was a freshman at Example High School. During the first semester of his freshmen year, he consistently made Cs or lower on his research papers for English class. Tommy would frequently get frustrated with writing research papers because he did not know how to find reliable information, and did not know how to structure and cite his work. Although he knew he would be expected to select and research a topic for his Senior Exit project, he did not think he would be able to do so, and did not think he would graduate. Tommy participated in the six-week research program facilitated by the public library. Librarians showed Tommy how to select a topic for research, how to use online databases to find reliable information, and how to properly write and cite sources within a research paper. Tommy researched and wrote a paper after the conclusion of the six-week library program and earned an A on his paper. Tommy has consistently made grades of Bs to As on all of his English research assignments. Most important, Tommy now feels that he can write his Senior Exit research paper, and that he will graduate in 2016.

In terms of youth at risk, a story of impact could look like the following:

1. *Person*—Example: Anthony was a bright, young thirteen-year-old boy.
2. *Problem*—Example: Anthony was a reluctant reader and was having trouble with reading comprehension. Anthony said that reading was not fun.
3. *Library intervention*—Example: Anthony's mom took him to the library, where he participated in the *Bone* graphic novel book club. Anthony got to meet author Jeff Smith at a library event, which inspired him to read the other books in the *Bone* series.
4. *Happy ending*—Example: Anthony's mom called last week, and he's doing much better in school. He is much more interested in reading, and has started reading books for fun.

LaRue urged libraries to "make the impact about the person, not ourselves." Rather than saying "I thought this was a great book for a patron who had a child with a disability, so I recommended it to him, and I was able to change their lives," a better example would be, "John was a patron who regularly came to us seeking information on his child's disability. He came to the library, we helped him find a book, and as a result his child was able to make significant progress" (LaRue, 2011). Stories of impact show stakeholders the individual connections libraries make with patrons. The at-risk community can potentially generate very powerful stories of impact that make a case for continual service. These examples, paired with library output measures and measurable outcomes, give library staff powerful data to share with stakeholders in the continual task of striving for service to the at-risk population. See the sidebar on pages 165–167 for an example of a report that could be submitted to decision makers after developing a program with measurable outcomes.

Conclusion

As previously stated, it is important for libraries to determine a measurable outcome before they begin a program. It is extremely difficult to link developmental changes within a population to a specific program unless one has the research, theory, and method to confirm the results. Unless a measurable outcome is articulated at the beginning of an initiative, the data gathered is irrelevant.

Working with and advocating for youth at risk is not a simple endeavor. At times, library staff may feel that they are not making a difference because the initiatives they facilitate are too small with a minimal impact. Library staff might feel insignificant in a large system of organizations serving at-risk youth and wonder if their programs are worth the effort. However, they should realize that for many of these teens, one person is all that is needed to encourage them to turn their lives around. Staff may not see the lasting impact of their programs on the adolescents with whom they work, but many of the teens will remember, and benefit from, their efforts.

References

Boudreau, Janine. 2011. "Outcomes Training: Charlotte Mecklenburg Library." Presentation for Charlotte Mecklenburg Library Managers by the United Way of Central Carolinas, Charlotte, NC, June 14, 2011.

LaRue, Jamie. 2011. "Who Speaks for Us? Library Advocacy." Presentation at workshops for Lyrasis and the State Library of North Carolina, Durham and Greensboro, NC, November 28 and 30.

Matthews, Joe. 2010. "Evaluating Summer Reading Programs: Suggested Improvements." *Public Libraries* 49, no. 4: 34–40. http://www.publiclibrariesonline.org/magazines/featured-articles/evaluating-summer-reading-programs-suggested-improvements.

Metz, Allison J. R. 2007. "Why Conduct a Program Evaluation? Five Reasons Why Evaluation Can Help an Out-of-School Time Program." *Research-to-Results Brief*, Publication #2007-31. Child Trends. http://www.childtrends.org/files/child_trends-2007_10_01_rb_whyprogeval.pdf.

APPENDIX A

Forms

This appendix collects the forms referenced throughout the text that are used by library staff for programs facilitated with youth at risk. The forms can be tailored as needed for the programs and teen populations of libraries' individual communities. Editable files are available for download at http://www.ala editions.org/webextras/.

Measurable Outcome and Evaluation Plan

Staff Responsible/Department: _____

Need:

Goal:

Outcome:

Target Population(s)	Theory	Input	Activities	Output

Source: This form is provided courtesy of Angela Craig.

Goal Development

Staff Responsible/Department: _____

Goal:				
Measurable Outcome(s)	**Implementation**	**Timeline**	**Evaluation Measures**	**Projected Outcomes**
				Initial outcome: **Intermediate outcome:** **Long-term outcome:**

Source: This form is provided courtesy of Angela Craig.

Stories of Impact

Staff Responsible/Department: _____

Story 1:				
Person	**Problem**	**Library Intervention**	**Happy Ending**	**Final Write-Up**

Story 2:				
Person	**Problem**	**Library Intervention**	**Happy Ending**	**Final Write-Up**

Source: This form is provided courtesy of Angela Craig.

Staff Assessment Form

Do you like teenagers?	Yes	No
Do you enjoy working with teens?	Yes	No
Do you feel you are easy to approach, and, if so, do you feel a teen would approach you?	Yes	No
Do you feel you are patient?	Yes	No
Can you work with a population that might push you outside your comfort zone?	Yes	No
Are you open to working with a population in an environment that is not the library, such as a detention center or alternative school?	Yes	No
Are you open to visiting environments teens frequent to encourage them to come to the library?	Yes	No
When working with this population, can you remain neutral about the teen's personal history, such as arrest records, involvement in gangs, substance abuse, pregnancy, and so forth?	Yes	No
Would you feel comfortable managing conflicts between adolescents?	Yes	No
Can you ensure the safety of the teens who participate in your programs?	Yes	No
Are you willing to spend extra time developing appropriate programs for this population, even if you have to use personal time?	Yes	No
Are you flexible, willing, and able to adapt to the needs of this population?	Yes	No
Are you motivated to pursue community partnerships that would benefit at-risk teens?	Yes	No
Are you willing to advocate for services to the at-risk population even if no one else within your library will do so?	Yes	No
Source: This form is provided courtesy of Angela Craig.		

Teen Volunteer Program: Application

Today's Date: _____

Last Name: _____   First Name: _____

Street Address: _____

City: _____   State: _____   Zip Code: _____

Home telephone: _____   Cell phone: _____

E-mail: _____

Age: _____   Date of Birth: _____   Gender: Male / Female

Emergency Contact: _____

School: _____

Grade Level: _____

Is this a community service requirement?   Yes / No

If yes, specify: _____ School   _____ Other   _____ Court Assigned

Do you have a specified number of hours you are required to complete? If so, list below:

Total number of hours needed: _____

To be completed by (date):   _____

Availability:

What day(s) are you able to volunteer? What hours are you interested in volunteering?

For example: Mon and Fri 3–5 or Mon and Sat 10–12

_____

Tell us why you would like to volunteer at the library.

_____

_____

_____

(Continued)

Teen Volunteer Program: Application *(Continued)*

Please tell us about any special skills you have or any areas of interest.

For example: technical skills (Word, PowerPoint, or Excel) or relevant past working experience (tutoring/volunteer work)

_____

_____

_____

_____

I understand that it is the Library's policy to protect the privacy of those who use the library. I agree to hold information about patrons in complete confidence and to access this information only in the course of performing my volunteer assignments. In addition, I understand that a breach of confidentiality is grounds for dismissal from the volunteer services program. I also understand that background checks may be necessary for some positions. My submission of this application to the library indicates an agreement with these terms and conditions.

Please note: Background checks are required for volunteers age 17 and over.

Signature: _____   Date: _____

Source: This form is provided courtesy of Librarian Tiffany Boeglen and Larisa Martin, Library Services Specialist, and the Charlotte Mecklenburg Library.

Teen Volunteer Program: Interview Questions

Candidate Name: _____   Age: _____   Grade Level: _____

School: _____

Do you have to fulfill a community service requirement for school?   Yes / No

If yes, date for completion: _____

Why are you interested in volunteering at the library?

_____

_____

_____

How did you hear about the library's teen volunteer program?

_____

_____

_____

Do you have a library card?   Yes / No

How often do you visit the library?

_____

What library volunteer activities are you interested in?

_____

_____

_____

Do you have any previous volunteer experience?

_____

_____

_____

What did you like most about your previous experiences?

_____

_____

_____

(Continued)

Teen Volunteer Program: Interview Questions *(Continued)*

What do you anticipate getting out of your volunteer experience with the library?

_____

_____

_____

Do you have any special skills you'd like to share that might make you stand out from the rest of the applicants?

_____

_____

_____

What are three words that best describe you?

1. _____

2. _____

3. _____

Technology-related interview questions:

(Rate comfort level on a scale of 1 to 10, 1 being not comfortable and 10 being very comfortable.)

___ Microsoft Word

___ Using digital camera/handheld video camera

___ Uploading photos to Flickr or comparable site

___ Using the library's online catalog to place holds

___ Laptop/DVD player, projector, and speakers (setting up for programming)

___ Wii, PS2, Xbox (setting up and also teaching other teens who may be less familiar)

Source: This form is provided courtesy of Librarian Tiffany Boeglen and Larisa Martin, Library Services Specialist, and the Charlotte Mecklenburg Library.

Teen Volunteer Program: Skills Assessment

Name: _____

E-mail/Phone Number: _____

Please answer the questions below. If asked, please rate your comfort level on a scale of 1 to 5, with 1 reflecting little to no experience and 5 very experienced.

1. Are you a library user?   Yes / No

2. Do you have a home branch?   Yes / No

3. Have you ever used our self-check-out system?

   Rate your comfort level: 1 2 3 4 5

4. Are you familiar with our online catalog?

   Rate your comfort level: 1 2 3 4 5

5. Are you familiar with our online databases? Adults'? Children's?

   Rate your comfort level: 1 2 3 4 5

6. Are you familiar with our PC reservation system that patrons use to book Internet time?

   Rate your comfort level: 1 2 3 4 5

7. Do you have any experience working with Microsoft Office products? Please list the software applications you are most comfortable using.

   Rate your comfort level: 1 2 3 4 5

8. Do you have any experience performing research both online and in the library? Please list any relevant qualifications.

   Rate your comfort level: 1 2 3 4 5

9. Do you have any experience working with children? Please list any relevant qualifications.

Source: This form was created by and provided courtesy of Emily Anne Leachman, Reference and Teen Services Librarian, Cabarrus County Public Library.

Teen Volunteer Program: Skills Assessment

Alphabetization Worksheet

Put the following authors' last names in alphabetical order:

Mason	DiTrelizzi
McMurty	D'Italiano
McMurphy	Ditko
Maine	Ditchfield, Mike
McDonald	Dispirito, Nicolina
Madison	DiStefano
Maby	Dister
Mains	DiSpezio
MacDonald	DiSpirito, Rocco
McVeigh	Ditchfield, Christian
Mazer	
Maines	

Source: This form was created by and provided courtesy of Emily Anne Leachman, Reference and Teen Services Librarian, Cabarrus County Public Library.

Teen Volunteer Program: Skills Assessment

Dewey Decimal System Exercise

Put the following numbers in correct Dewey Decimal order:

311.0942

311.116

311.2

310.101

311.07

310.018

311.018

311.126

310.3

Source: This form was created by and provided courtesy of Emily Anne Leachman, Reference and Teen Services Librarian, Cabarrus County Public Library.

Library Partnership Evaluation

Did the program contribute to the objectives?

    QUITE A LOT   A LOT   JUST A LITTLE   NOT AT ALL

How would you rate the program?

    EXCELLENT   GOOD   POOR   VERY POOR

Length of program:

    JUST RIGHT   TOO SHORT   TOO LONG

Was the library staff encouraging?

    QUITE A LOT   A LOT   JUST A LITTLE   NOT AT ALL

Was the library staff clear in their communication?

    QUITE A LOT   A LOT   JUST A LITTLE   NOT AT ALL

In your opinion, how much did the residents enjoy the program?

    QUITE A LOT   A LOT   JUST A LITTLE   NOT AT ALL

Do you have any activity ideas for the library to incorporate into a future program?

_____

_____

Do you have any suggestions for program themes or topics of interest among the students?

_____

_____

Do you have any suggestions for program themes or topics of interest among the students?

_____

_____

How can library staff be more encouraging and helpful to the residents?

_____

_____

Additional Comments:

_____

_____

Source: This form is provided courtesy of Laura Kauffman and the Lancaster Public Library.

Evaluation for Teen Participants

Program Name: _____

What did you most enjoy about the program?

_____

_____

Is there a part of the program that you did not like?

_____

_____

Did you learn anything new because of the program? If so, what was it?

_____

_____

How much did you read before you started coming to library programs?

     None   A little   Once a week   More than once a week   All the time

How much did you read after you started coming to library programs?

     None   A little   Once a week   More than once a week   All the time

What would you like the library to bring to you?

_____

_____

Anything else you want to say?

_____

_____

Source: This form is provided courtesy of Angela Craig and the Charlotte Mecklenburg Library.

Teen Parent Exit Form: Baby Program

1. Parent's Name: _____
   E-mail: _____

2. How many storytime classes did you attend?

0–2	7–10
2–5	10+
5–7	

3. Have you attended similar programs here or at another location?   Yes / No

4. Has storytime encouraged you to spend more time reading to your child?
   Yes / No

5. Since participating in storytime, how important do you believe it is to read to your child?

   Extremely   Somewhat   Not Important

6. Has storytime encouraged you to sing or rhyme with your child?   Yes / No

7. Has your communication with your child changed since being in this class?
   Yes / No

8. Do you feel more confident now choosing a book for your child?   Yes / No

9. At this time, how many children's books do you have at home?

1–2 books	26–50 books
3–10 books	51 books or more
11–25 books	

10. About how often do you read books or stories to your children?

Never	Several times a month
Several times a year	Once a week
About 3 times a week	Every day

(Continued)

Teen Parent Exit Form: Baby Program *(Continued)*

11. When you read to your children, do you . . . (Please respond YES or NO.)

    See your baby play with books?   Yes / No

    Read the same story over and over?   Yes / No

    Talk about the pictures in the book?   Yes / No

12. Name an early literacy (prereading) skill: _____

13. Please respond YES or NO.

    Does your child enjoy reading time?   Yes / No

    Does your child know how to use a book?   Yes / No

    Does your child recognize different shapes?   Yes / No

    Do you rhyme with your child?   Yes / No

    Do you talk to your baby in parentese or baby talk?   Yes / No

14. Here is a list of some things that people may read. Please tell me whether you
    have read any of the materials during the past week.
    (Please respond YES or NO.)

    Online reading: blogs, journals, magazines (not Facebook)   Yes / No

    Books   Yes / No

    Magazines   Yes / No

    Information sent from a teacher or school/homework assignments   Yes / No

15. Name one new thing you learned from this program.

    _____

16. What did you like best about this program?

    _____

17. What did you like least about this program?

    _____

Source: This form is provided courtesy of Anna Hartman, Children's Librarian, San Diego
County Library–La Mesa Branch, and Kirby McCurtis, Youth Librarian, San Diego Public Library.

Organizations That Serve Youth

The organizations listed here represent partnership opportunities for libraries that wish to serve at-risk youth. The list includes those organizations that teens can join and organizations that make public policy regarding youth at risk. The institutions listed are national organizations, and in addition to these, libraries can look for local branches of the organizations and seek opportunities with their community groups. Libraries can connect with these organizations and gain a foothold within the at-risk population as well as facilitate much-needed programs to the teens that they serve.

As discussed in Chapter 1, staff should ensure that the organization is both in line with the library mission and also supports the diversity of the at-risk population. A successful collaboration is contingent upon the library and its partnered organization being in agreement regarding the needs of youth at risk and how best to serve them. Libraries will want to research youth associations and solicit support and partnerships from like-minded organizations that will be inclusive of all teens. An effective community partnership offers many possibilities for collaboration and teamwork that can greatly enhance the lives of at-risk teens.

National Organizations

Big Brothers Big Sisters of America
http://www.bbbs.org/
This national organization partners children and adults for one-on-one inter-actions. The adults who are part of the organization serve as role models, mentors, and friends to the youth in their care.

Boy Scouts of America
http://www.scouting.org/
This national organization strives to build character, foster citizenship, and support the development of youth within the context of adventure, explora-tion, and fun. BSA also has programs that specifically target the at-risk popu-lation in both rural and urban communities.

Boys and Girls Clubs of America
http://www.bgca.org/
As stated on their website, the goal of the Boys and Girls Clubs of America is "to enable all young people, especially those who need us most, to reach their full potential as productive, caring, responsible citizens."

Camp Fire
http://www.campfireusa.org/
This organization focuses on fostering youth skills, along with personal and social development, and also strives to incorporate and promote diversity with the teens that utilize its activities.

Girl Scouts of the USA
http://www.girlscouts.org/
The Girl Scouts organization promotes the educational growth and development of girls aged five to seventeen. Many leadership and skill-building opportunities are available for participants. The organization has worked to increase its out-reach efforts to communities with greater racial and economic diversity.

Girls on the Run
http://www.girlsontherun.org/
This experiential program is for girls aged eight to thirteen years old and combines training for a 3.1-mile running event with self-esteem-enhancing,

uplifting workouts. The goal of the organization is to "encourage positive emotional, social, mental, spiritual, and physical development and to educate and empower girls at an early age in order to prevent the display of at-risk activities in the future."

National 4-H Clubs
http://www.4-h.org/
This organization provides hands-on learning, research-based youth programs, and adult mentorship that promote the development of life skills. In recent years, 4-H clubs have worked to incorporate more initiatives that target at-risk youth. Many excellent and free training opportunities are available for staff that help promote fiscal awareness, science, citizenship, and healthy living.

YMCA
http://www.ymca.net/
Many of the local YMCA branches offer programs that support youth at risk. The YMCA focuses on building self-esteem, character development, and personal skills and typically is an excellent community resource for teens and teen-serving organizations.

Organizations That Create Public Policy and Disseminate Information

America's Promise Alliance
http://www.americaspromise.org/
This organization coordinates more than 400 national partner organizations and their local affiliates. Ensuring that all young people graduate from high school and are ready for college, work, and life is a top priority of the organization. Other initiatives focus on action being taken at the community level to improve the well-being of young people across the nation.

Bureau for At-Risk Youth
http://www.at-risk.com/
The bureau publishes and provides guidance and prevention materials for K–12 schools as well as youth service and juvenile justice organizations. The organization is an excellent resource for educators, counselors, parents, and youth-serving organizations.

Center for Youth Studies
http://www.centerforyouth.org/
The mission of the Center for Youth Studies is to provide relevant and current informational resources and to promote global collaboration toward a comprehensive systems approach to ministry with youth. This organization strives to be an interactive partner with youth workers both locally and around the world, providing information resources to practitioners and parents and research assistance for students and professors.

Child Welfare League of America
http://www.cwla.org/
CWLA is a coalition of hundreds of private and public agencies serving vulnerable children and families. The organization focuses on children and youth who may have experienced abuse, neglect, family disruption, or a range of other factors that jeopardize their safety, permanence, or well-being. CWLA also supports the families, caregivers, and communities that care for and work with these children.

FHI 360 Center for Youth Development and Engagement
http://cydpr.aed.org/
As stated on their website, this organization is "a national capacity-building intermediary that seeks to create and strengthen the infrastructures that support the positive development of all youth in America. . . . [T]he Center's fundamental approach is to work with local, state, and national partners in order to help build and invest in a youth development infrastructure, which includes data collection and analysis, capacity and community-building, and educational issues."

National Network for Youth
http://www.nn4youth.org/
This organization advocates for the needs of runaway, homeless, and other disconnected youth. They have extensive member organizations that are community-based, along with connections to neighborhood youth, adults, associations, and regional and state networks of youth workers.

Core Titles for Youth at Risk

YA Urban Life

Bailey-Williams, Nicole. *The Love Child's Revenge*. New York: Broadway Books, 2008. ISBN: 978-0767919111.

> Claudia Fryar, a quiet product of an adulterous relationship—a love child—gets teased by other children and mistreated by adults. She leaves home after her dad dies. Things spin out of control when her dad's envious widow takes her for her inheritance. Claudia gets tired of being stepped on and goes through a dramatic makeover. She even changes her name to Peach Harrison after she graduates from college. Peach becomes a successful journalist who returns home for revenge. Does Peach get what is owed to her?

Booth, Coe. *Bronxwood*. New York: Push, 2011. ISBN: 978-0439925341.

> Tyrell is fifteen years old with full adult responsibilities. He is broke and struggling to take care of his seven-year-old brother Troy. Their mother relies on social services and their father is in and out of jail. When they are evicted from their Bronx project apartment everything goes downhill. Tyrell comes up with a plan to get his family an apartment. Will holding down his family cause him to end up in jail like his father?

Buckhanon, Kalisha. *Upstate*. New York: St. Martin's Press, 2006. ISBN: 978-0312332693.

> Antonio and Natasha, two teens in love, are faced with challenges that test their faith. Antonio is accused of a serious crime and gets locked up. As he

struggles to stay alive while in jail, Natasha goes through major situations that change her life. They stay in touch over the years and wonder if they will ever be together again.

Daniels, Babygirl. *16½ on the Block*. West Babylon, NY: Urban Books, 2009. ISBN: 978-1601621832.

Latina Smith and her homegirls, Asia and Gena, think it is all about them. They are the most popular girls in Cass High School. Everyone envies their high school lifestyle. Latina's home life is anything but the best; her mom is an addict, she lives in Detroit's projects, and she wants nothing more than to have a different life. Her reputation changes when the hating, lying, and jealousy takes over. She has twenty-four hours to save her own life and is unsure if she will be able do it.

Dotson-Lewis, Gloria. *Ninety-Nine Problems*. East Orange, NJ: W. Clark, 2011. ISBN: 978-1936649426.

Crea and Fiona are best friends for life until Fiona's new attraction for a drug dealer changes things. Crea has to deal with her secret crush on Brandon, the issues with her brother's depression and trouble after their father dies. Fiona loves the bad boys, but is Romero more than she can handle? Will Crea and Fiona remain BFFs?

King, Deja. *Ride Wit' Me*. Collierville, TN: A King Production, 2009. ISBN: 978-0975581193.

Mercedes and Dalvin are two young lovers from two different worlds. Dalvin, a young hustler, and Mercedes, a daddy's girl, fall for each other. Mercedes does not ever disappoint her father until Dalvin steals her heart.

McDonald, Janet. *Harlem Hustle*. New York: Frances Foster Books/Farrar, Straus and Giroux, 2006. ISBN: 978-0374371845.

Most teenage boys in New York City aspire to be rappers. Eric (Hustle) is left to fend for himself and discovers that surviving in the streets isn't easy. After serving time in jail, he attempts to get his rap dream off the ground all while he makes a quick buck shoplifting and selling the goods. As he tries to stay out of jail, a record producer bamboozles him and he realizes that school is important.

McDonald, Janet. *Twists and Turns*. New York: Farrar, Straus and Giroux, 2006. ISBN: 978-0374400064.

Teesha and Keeba are sisters who view life differently. The twins finally graduate from high school and need to figure out what to do next. A librarian convinces them that they have a talent for braiding hair and encourages them to open a beauty parlor. With TeeKee's Tresses up and running in the "hood," they soon realize that they must work together to overcome life's complicated twist and turns.

Simone, Ni-Ni. *Shortie Like Mine*. New York: Kensington Publishing, 2008. ISBN: 978-0758228390.

Even though sixteen-year-old Seven McKnight is beautiful, fly, and fabulous, she is the thickest girl in her crew and has issues. Not only is Seven hiding that her twin sister Toi is dating the neighborhood hustler, she is also in love with her high-maintenance homegirl Deeyah's boyfriend. Josiah is the flyest boy in school and she can't ignore her feelings for him. Deeyah causes drama between Josiah and his worst enemy. As the drama continues, can Seven try and set things right or does she end up trying to save herself from major heartbreak?

Simone, Ni-Ni. *Upgrade U*. New York: Dafina Books, 2011. ISBN: 978-0758241917.

Shae, Khya, and Seven are college freshmen excited about what the environment of higher education has to offer. They soon find out that life is poppin' in college. Seven is wifey of the hottest baller at Stiles University. With groupies threatening her basketball wife status and Josiah's hopes of an NBA career making his head big, Seven finds herself crushing on Zaire, a fine sophomore. Zaire's been checking out Seven for a while, waiting for his chance to step to her. Josiah has big-man status on campus and everyone loves him. A girl who keeps hanging around him has Seven feeling jealous and insecure, especially when he ignores her texts. She finds herself falling for Zaire and as she decides to give Zaire her everything, Josiah becomes determined to win Seven back.

Prison, Gangs, and Teen Violence

Binns, B. A. *Pull*. Lodi, NJ: WestSide Books, 2010. ISBN: 978-1934813430.

High school senior David Albacore's father kills his mother. After this tragedy, he changes his name and moves to a tough inner-city neighborhood. David blames himself for not saving his mother's life that night. With his mother gone and father in jail, he tries to care for his sisters.

Brown, Jennifer. *Hate List*. New York: Little, Brown, 2009.
ISBN: 978-0316041447.

> Valerie Leftman's boyfriend, Nick, opens fire in their school's cafeteria. Valerie saves the life of a wounded classmate but is accused of being involved in the shootings because she helped Nick create a list of people and things that he hated. Did she know he was going to use the list to pick his targets?

Dean, Carolee. *Take Me There*. New York: Simon Pulse, 2010.
ISBN: 978-1416989509.

> Seventeen-year-old Dylan Dawson is a troubled teen involved in gang activity. It doesn't matter how hard he tries to avoid trouble, it always finds him. He believes he inherited the trouble trait from his father, who is in jail facing death by lethal injection. Jess, a girl that he falls in love with, gives him the courage to overcome the obstacles in his life.

Elkeles, Simone. *Chain Reaction*. New York: Walker and Company, 2011.
ISBN: 978-0802720870.

> Luis Fuentes has always been sheltered from the reality of gang violence until it almost destroys his brothers' lives. This doesn't mean he isn't a risk-taker. Luis will do anything for the next big thrill.

Hamilton, Steve. *The Lock Artist*. New York: Minotaur Books, 2010.
ISBN 978-0312380427.

> Mike experiences something bad when he is eight, and he has not said a word in ten years. He goes to jail and then decides to tell his story. In his junior year in high school, Mike discovers that he has a talent for picking locks.

Hilton, David E. *Kings of Colorado*. New York: Simon and Schuster Paperbacks, 2012. ISBN: 978-1439183830.

> William Sheppard, fifteen, is sent away to the Swope Ranch Boys' Reformatory, after stabbing his abusive father in the chest. His father lives and Will spends two years at the reformatory for protecting his mother. The boys at the camp have to decide to trust one another and make a family or be alone to face life locked up. Will quickly learns who are his friends and who are not!

Hunter, Travis. *Two the Hard Way*. New York: Kensington Publishing, 2010.
ISBN: 978-0758242501.

> Seventeen-year-old Romeo Braxton admired his big brother but wasn't going end up like him; he plans to go to college to play football. Kwame

was serving two years in prison for something he didn't do. Everyone in their Atlanta projects knew he was innocent. Kwame took the rap for his friend, who asked for a favor, when the cops showed up and found bags of weed and white in the truck. Kwame didn't open his mouth; his loyalty to the streets caused him two years of his life. Kwame and Grandma loved Romeo and weren't going let him make the same mistake.

Kowalski, William. *The Barrio Kings.* Victoria, BC/Custer, WA: Raven Books, 2010. ISBN: 978-1554692446.

Rosario tries to move past his banger days after his brother was murdered in a gang fight. His girlfriend is pregnant with his first son; he's trying to finish his GED; and he's working hard to get a promotion at the super-market. He wishes his gang-banging past would go away but it doesn't. Rosario's pregnant girlfriend is hit in a drive-by shooting, which forces him to make some tough decisions.

Kuklin, Susan. *No Choirboy: Murder, Violence, and Teenagers on Death Row.* New York: Henry Holt, 2008. ISBN: 978-0805079500.

No Choirboy looks into the lives of teenage inmates inside America's prisons. They tell real stories about life in jail, sharing their thoughts and feelings about how they ended up behind bars.

Myers, Walter Dean. *Locked Down.* New York: Amistad, 2011. ISBN: 978-0061214820.

Reese, fourteen, got locked up in a juvenile facility for stealing a drug prescription pad, and the only chance he sees of getting out is going from juvy to real jail. He wants to get out early, but a problem comes up, and he has to decide if he will help his friend Toon or not; if he does, it may cost him his freedom. What will Reese do?

Read, Cornelia. *The Crazy School.* New York: Grand Central, 2010. ISBN: 978-0446198202.

Madeline Dare works as a teacher at a boarding school for emotionally troubled teens. One of her students commits suicide, but she thinks it may have been murder, as someone tries to kill her.

Rodríguez, Luis J. *It Calls You Back: An Odyssey through Love, Addiction, Revolutions, and Healing.* New York: Simon and Schuster, 2011. ISBN: 978-1416584162.

The sequel to *Always Running* starts at the end of Rodríguez's jail sentence as a teenager. He struggles to stop his heroin addiction, get clean, obtain a job, and take care of his children. Rodriguez soon discovers his talents as a writer and realizes that the past always comes back to haunt you. His oldest son is sent to prison for attempted murder and Rodríguez has to step up to the plate as a father and stand up for his son.

Smith, Alexander Gordon. *Death Sentence: Escape from Furnace #3*. New York: Square Fish, 2012. ISBN: 978-0312674410.

Furnace Penitentiary is a tough place to be and Alex tries to escape twice. He faces a harder punishment this time, and he turns into a raging monster in the bloodstained facilities in the basement. He is given drugs by the warden and becomes insane. Alex is scared to death of what he has become. Will he be able to regain his sanity and break away from the evil that was embedded in him, in order to free himself from the torture of prison?

Gay, Lesbian, Bisexual, and Transgender

Beam, Cris. *I Am J*. New York: Little, Brown, 2011. ISBN: 978-0316053617.

J is a half-Jewish, half–Puerto Rican teen who was born a girl. His parents were always supportive and encouraged him to do well in school. They thought J was a lesbian, but they didn't know that J is a boy in a girl's body. He knows his parents will not be happy when they find out he has been taking testosterone shots and wants to fully transition. J undergoes therapy for two weeks in order to get permission to legally change into what he has always been—a boy. Through a support group, J learns more about being transgender, the GLBTQ community, and himself.

Belgue, Nancy. *Soames on the Range*. New York: HarperCollins Children's Books, 2011. ISBN: 978-0002007689.

Soames grew up in an abnormal family in San Francisco: his parents were hippies and his twin sisters get into a lot of trouble. However, nothing is worse to him than finding out that his father is gay.

Berman, Steve, ed. *Speaking Out: LGBTQ Youth Stand Up*. Valley Falls, NY: Bold Strokes Books, 2011. ISBN: 978-1602825666.

This is a collection of stories of young LGBT or Q teens that support the "It Gets Better" campaign.

Donley, Jan. *The Side Door.* Midway, FL: Spinsters Ink, 2010.
ISBN: 978-1935226123.

> Alex Weber's death has never been discussed by anyone—not at school or in the town he grew up in. Mel and her best friend Frank try to figure out why Alex killed himself. Mel finds something in the pocket of a pair of Alex's old pants that explains it all. She tries to tell the story of Alex's death, but no one wants to listen. She faces situations with courage and will get someone's attention no matter what it takes, even if she does so wrongfully.

Farrey, Brian. *With or Without You.* New York: Simon Pulse, 2011.
ISBN: 978-1442406995.

> Evan and Davis are high school graduates, planning to attend Madison College in Chicago. They have been friends since age ten and share a special relationship as a result of being teased, bullied, and abused because they are gay. Things change for them over the summer. Evan and Erik become more serious and Davis gets involved with the Chasers. As the summer goes on, Evan is faced with making some difficult choices about his future.

Hopkins, Ellen. *Perfect.* New York: Margaret K. McElderry Books, 2011.
ISBN: 978-1416983248.

> *Perfect* is a great follow-up for the book *Impulse.* Cara, Kendra, Sean, and Andre want to be perfect and each of them try different things to get there. Cara struggles with her sexuality, Kendra aspires to be a model and will do anything for a perfect image, Sean is a jock and wants to perfect his baseball game, and Andre wants a perfect career. The problem is, nothing is perfect.

Mourian, Tomas. *Hidden.* New York: Kensington Publishing, 2011.
ISBN: 978-0758251312.

> This is the story of a gay teenager, Amad, who is forced to undergo reparative therapy at Serenity Ridge, an abusive residential treatment program. He runs away from his homophobic parents and the program to an underground safe house in San Francisco for gay and transgender youth in danger.

Reardon, Robin. *A Question of Manhood.* New York: Kensington Publishing, 2010. ISBN: 978-0758246790.

> Sixteen-year-old Paul's older brother Chris is his role model and serves in the Army during the Vietnam war. Paul has always admired his brother and is anxious for him to come home for good. When Chris comes home for a quick visit, he tells Paul that he is gay. Chris returns to war and is killed,

leaving Paul grieving with the burden of a secret he can't share. Should Paul tell someone to lift the weight off his shoulders?

Sanchez, Alex. *Boyfriends with Girlfriends*. New York: Simon and Schuster BFYR, 2011. ISBN: 978-1416937739.

Lance is seventeen years old and is searching for his first love. He thought he had found love with Sergio, a guy on the high school swim team, but he was wrong. He connects with Sergio online and they really like each other, but Lance doesn't know if he should continue to pursue the relationship because Sergio is bisexual. Lance doesn't know if someone can actually be bisexual. He thinks that people can only be straight or gay, not both.

Savage, Dan, and Terry Miller. *It Gets Better: Coming Out, Overcoming Bullying, and Creating a Life Worth Living*. New York: Dutton, 2011. ISBN: 978-0525952336.

This is a collection of essays that discusses the effects of social media on the LGBT teen community, such as when the news causes an LGBT teen to commit suicide. The authors try to advise teens that school is the key to their success, and that no matter what happens to them life will eventually get better.

Homeless Youth, Runaways, and Teens from Disconnected Families

Adams, Lenora. *Baby Girl*. New York: Simon Pulse, 2007. ISBN: 978-1416925125.

Sheree is pregnant again and weighed down by the emotional burden of her mother's smoking and sexual promiscuity, Ange's abortion, her father's abandonment, and the twenty-five-year-old drug-dealing father of her baby who has taken her heart and self-worth. She runs away and writes her mother a letter explaining her reasons for leaving. Sheree's mother responds with a letter asking her to come home to get help raising her new baby.

Clark, Margaret. *Care Factor Zero*. New York: Avon Tempest, 2000. ISBN: 978-0380813902.

Larceny is a wild girl. She's been to many different foster homes, harassed by the cops, and lived on the streets. She is afraid of being confined by walls and bars, which is why she's on the streets in the first place. She hears voices that make her act crazy wild with a rage to kill.

Griffin, Paul. *Ten Mile River.* New York: Speak, 2011. ISBN: 978-0142419830.

Two teenage boys escape from a juvenile detention center and foster care to live in an abandoned shack in a New York City park. They make a living stealing, hustling, and occasionally working to keep from being arrested and sent back into the system.

Moses, Shelia P. *Joseph's Grace.* New York: Margaret K. McElderry Books, 2011. ISBN: 978-1416939429.

Joseph Flood has a busy life as his sophomore year begins. He has school, work, tennis, and a new girlfriend, Valerie. His father requests that he go to live with his aunt and uncle to get away from his drug-addicted mother. Joseph's older cousin Jasmine is shot by his mother's sometime boyfriend. Jasmine was the shining star of the family and everyone expected her to make it out of the hood. Joseph and his aunt and uncle struggle hard to accept Jasmine's death while attempting to get his mother clean.

Yansky, Brian. *Wonders of the World.* Woodbury, MN: Flux, 2007. ISBN: 978-0738710846.

Eric runs away from his home in Omaha and lives on the streets in Riverton, Nebraska. Eric and his friends Catgirl and Payback get into drugs, prostitution, and revenge. Eric realizes that he likes acting and begins to explore a local play that changes his life. His talents and ambitions save him from the streets and death, unlike his friends.

Teens and Pregnancy

Bechard, Margaret. *Hanging on to Max.* New York: Simon Pulse, 2003. ISBN: 978-0689862687.

When his girlfriend wants to give their baby up for adoption, Sam becomes a single, sixteen-year-old father determined to keep and raise his newborn alone.

Bell, William. *Death Wind.* Victoria, BC/Custer, WA: Orca Book Publishers, 2002. ISBN: 978-1551432151.

Allie is failing in school and fears that she is pregnant by her ex-boyfriend. She decides that it is way too complicated to face her always-fighting parents and runs away. She gains appreciation for life when a tornado rips through her town, destroying her home and injuring her mom.

Buckhanon, Kalisha. *Conception*. New York: St. Martin's Press, 2008. ISBN: 978-0312332709.

> Growing up in Chicago, fifteen-year-old Shivana believes in the perception that all black women are the same: single, broke, and alone raising kids, like her mother. She wishes for a life better than what she sees around her and does not know how to get it. She has no real role models other than her beautiful, entertaining, enthusiastic Aunt Jewel, who comes to visit once in a while, and the older man in her building who uses her. When Shivana discovers that she is pregnant by the older man, she must decide what to do. As she begins her journey toward adulthood, she meets Rasul, another troubled teen, who gives her hope and complicates her decisions. Together they fight to overcome the challenges and push for a more positive future.

Buckley, Kate. *Choices*. Bothell: WA: Book Publishers Network, 2009. ISBN: 978-1935359128.

> Teens face all kinds of challenges: underage drinking, rape, abuse, family secrets, and abortion. Fifteen-year-old Kara, a sophomore at an all-girls Catholic school in Colorado, finds herself facing a serious decision after one crazy night of partying. She experiences many emotions when her boyfriend dumps her after the pregnancy test comes back positive.

Burgess, Melvin. *Smack*. New York: Square Fish, 2010. ISBN: 978-0312608620.

> Fourteen-year-old Tar decides he does not want to continue being abused by his father and runs away with his girlfriend, Gemma. They become friends with other homeless people who introduce them to the fast life and the drugs that they quickly become addicted to. Gemma gets pregnant and after three years living a chaotic life of drugs, prostitution, and robbery, she is forced to go back home with her new daughter.

Connelley Worlton, Stephanie. *Hope's Journey*. Springville, UT: Bonneville Books, 2011. ISBN: 978-1599555065.

> Sydney is going to college on a scholarship and Alex a jock preparing to serve on a Latter Day Saints mission. The night after their high school graduation, all of their hopes and dreams for the future come crashing down when they discover that Sydney is pregnant. They must increase their faith in God to help them through the separation and confusion.

Efaw, Amy. *After*. New York: Viking, 2009. ISBN: 9780670011834.

> Devon is a talented, athletic, teenage girl with a future heading toward the Olympics as a soccer player. How could she end up throwing her newborn baby in the trash right after giving birth? The police search the apartment building looking for evidence regarding an abandoned baby. When they reach Devon's apartment, her mother, just getting home from the night shift at Safeway, opens the door and informs the officer that her daughter is sick and stayed home from school. The officer connects being sick with the newborn baby and things go haywire from there. Devon is thrown into a world so unfamiliar to her with kids with problems she never imagined. She is stuck in a juvenile detention facility, under twenty-four-hour surveillance, without anyone.

Grant, Cynthia D. *The White Horse*. New York: Aladdin Paperbacks, 1998. ISBN: 9780689832635.

> Raina reveals the pains of her life to a concerned teacher through her writings. At sixteen years old, her troubles with a dysfunctional family, life on the streets, drug abuse, and an unplanned pregnancy are too much to handle alone.

Teen Relationship Abuse, Suicide, Sexual Childhood Abuse

Chaltas, Thalia. *Because I Am Furniture*. New York: Viking, 2009. ISBN: 9780670062980.

> Anke's father is abusive to everyone in her family except her. She is invisible in the chaotic household where she witnesses the horror of her brother and sister getting beaten. She wishes she could disappear for real. When Anke makes the volleyball team at school, her confidence grows and she learns that if she says something, someone will hear her. Now that she knows people can see and hear her, will her voice ever be loud enough to save everyone in her house—including her—from her father's abuse?

Fehlbaum, Beth. *Hope in Patience*. Lodi, NJ: WestSide Books, 2010. ISBN: 9781934813416.

> Fifteen-year-old Ashley Asher has been sexually abused by her stepfather for years, but when she tells her mother, she doesn't believe her. Child Protective Services finally takes Ashley from her home after she is hurt so

badly that she ends up in the emergency room. She moves to Patience, Texas, to live with her real father and his new family, who she doesn't really know. Her new life is much better, but Ashley has a hard time trusting anyone. She sometimes scratches herself until she bleeds. Ashley is in therapy, but still remembers the pain of her past. Will she ever heal?

Peters, Julie Anne. *By the Time You Read This, I'll Be Dead*. New York: Hyperion, 2011. ISBN: 978-1423130215.

Daelyn is frustrated and tired of being bullied, teased, and hurt. She tries to commit suicide, but can't do it. She goes online and finds a site that helps her plan her suicide, and in twenty-three days, she will do it again, but this time it will work. She begins the countdown to her death and starts to say goodbye to everything in her life. She tries her best not to make any new friends and doesn't want to expose her plan. A boy tries to befriend her; she pushes him away. Will he be able to get inside and save Daelyn's life?

Rainfield, Cheryl. *Scars*. Lodi, NJ: WestSide Books, 2011. ISBN: 978-1934813577.

Kendra, fifteen, cannot stop thinking about the devastating memories of being sexually abused as a child. She never feels safe, especially since she cannot remember who her abuser was. Kendra is scared and paranoid; she thinks someone is always watching her and believes that they are leaving deranged messages that only she understands. Kendra copes with the pain through her beautiful artwork, but also by cutting herself. Since her mother is too self-centered to hear or see that she needs help, Kendra finds support in others. Soon the truth about Kendra's childhood abuse will be revealed with unexpected consequences.

Simone, Ni-Ni. *Teenage Love Affair*. New York: Dafina, 2010. ISBN: 978-0758241894.

Every Friday night Zsa-Zsa's father got drunk, abused her mother, and wouldn't stop until she called the police. Zsa-Zsa is programmed into thinking this behavior is normal. She dates Ameen, who is just like her father. He beats her if he thinks anything is wrong. Her friends and family try to help her get out, but she just can't because she is in love with Ameen. Zsa-Zsa's childhood love, Malichi, comes back on the scene and she knows he really cares for her. Will Zsa-Zsa let Malichi save her from her shameless love affair or will their friendship end?

Graphic Novels

Carey, Percy. *Sentences: The Life of M. F. Grimm.* New York: DC Comics, 2008. ISBN: 978-1401210472.

> This is the story of M. F. Grimm's life as a hip-hop grand master. It goes from the first time he picked up the microphone at a block party, to the day he got shot up and became paralyzed, to the time he spent in jail.

Lijewski, Christy. *Re:Play.* Hamburg/Los Angeles: TokyoPop, 2006. ISBN: 978-1598167375.

> Izsak is a homeless teen living underground in the subway, playing his guitar for money. Cree approaches him and asks him to join her band. She invites him to her home to meet her friend and bandmate. Rail thinks Izsak is strange but talented and lets him join the group. As time goes on, they discover that he is being stalked by a secret society of supernatural beings.

Eating Disorders

Bell, Julia. *Massive.* New York: Simon Pulse, 2003. ISBN: 978-1416902072.

> Carmen struggles with being overweight while her mother is obsessed with losing weight. Her mother suffers from an eating disorder, and Carmen decides to try eating and purging, which only leads her to become bulimic and paranoid. Carmen's health rapidly deteriorates as she becomes anorexic.

Bowman, Grace. *Thin.* London: Penguin, 2008. ISBN: 978-0141022840.

> Why would Grace Bowman try to kill herself at the age of eighteen? How did she make it? An anorexic teen, Grace is faced with the devastating decision of life or death, and shows that it is possible to overcome eating disorders and addiction.

Halse Anderson, Laurie. *Wintergirls.* New York: Viking, 2009. ISBN: 978-0670011100.

> Lia and Cassie are teenagers bonded by the secrets of anorexia. Cassie dies leaving Lia alone to face life without anyone to confide in. Lia's divorced parents fight over how to help her, her stepmother doesn't know what to do, and no one realizes that she is going through a mental breakdown. Will Lia die like Cassie did?

Kaslik, Ibi. *Skinny*. New York: Walker and Company, 2006.
ISBN: 978-0802796080.

> Giselle, a medical student and role model for her little sister Holly, struggles with anorexia. Holly, a track star, tries hard to keep her life together while dealing with the mental and physical breakdown of her sister.

Newman, LesLéa. *Fat Chance*. New York: PaperStar Books, 1996.
ISBN: 978-0698114067.

> Judi thinks she's fat and is convinced that she would be happy if she were skinnier. She writes about being thin in her diary, but when she becomes close friends with pencil-skinny Nancy Pratt, she learns a life-changing secret. Judi joins Nancy on the journey of bulimia. Judi's life spins out of control as her obsession with food, calories, and pounds becomes a matter of life and death.

Stewart, Maureen. *All of Me*. Ringwood, VIC: Puffin Books, 1996.
ISBN: 978-0140377712.

> Rebecca is fourteen years old and always dieting. She comes close to weighing thirty-five kilos/seventy-seven pounds, a goal she set for herself. Rebecca tries to remain in control of her weight loss addiction but can't. Her obsession gets so out of hand that she begins starving, taking laxatives, hiding food, and vomiting, nearly killing herself.

Nonfiction Self-Help Guides for Adults and Teens

Belge, Kathy, and Marke Bieschke. *Queer: The Ultimate LGBT Guide for Teens*. San Francisco, CA: Zest Books, 2011. ISBN: 978-0981973340.

> This guide provides teens with healthy advice about sex and coming out.

Bode, Janet. *Kids Still Having Kids: Talking about Teen Pregnancy*. Danbury, CT: Franklin Watts, 1999. ISBN: 978-0531159736.

> This book is a compilation of emotional teenage experiences, combined with statistical facts and advice. It presents interviews with teenage mothers and provides information about adoption, parenting, abortion, and foster care.

Corinna, Heather. *S.E.X.: The All-You-Need-to-Know Progressive Sexuality Guide to Get You through High School and College*. Cambridge, MA: Da Capo Press, 2007. ISBN: 978-1600940101.

This informational guide for teens about sexually transmitted diseases and infections includes a full bibliography of recommended sources.

Hasler, Nikol. *Sex: A Book for Teens: An Uncensored Guide to Your Body, Sex, and Safety*. San Francisco, CA: Zest Books, 2010. ISBN: 978-0981973326.

This question-and-answer guide for teens covers all aspects of sexuality and sexual orientation, masturbation, birth control, pregnancy, and diseases. The questions asked are those that teenagers do not dare to ask their parents.

Heller, Tania. *Pregnant! What Can I Do? A Guide for Teenagers*. Jefferson, NC: McFarland and Company, 2002. ISBN: 978-0786411696.

This book offers advice and guidance to pregnant teenagers, explaining the options of adoption, parenting, and abortion. It includes interviews with teens who share their personal experiences, discussion of the role of a father, information regarding planned parenthood and pregnancy prevention, and a list of resources.

McCafferty, Megan. *Sixteen: Stories about That Sweet and Bitter Birthday*. New York: Three Rivers Press, 2004. ISBN: 978-1400052707.

This collection of short stories is about being sixteen and addresses issues from getting a driver's license to dealing with teen pregnancy.

Westheimer, Ruth K., and Lehu, Pierre. *Dr. Ruth's Guide to Teens and Sex Today: From Social Networking to Friends with Benefits*. New York: Teachers College Press, 2008. ISBN: 978-1400052707.

This is an instructional book for parents and teens that focuses on sex, Internet safety, masturbation, and even friends with benefits.

Index

About the Authors

Angela Craig is originally from Texas and has worked with the at-risk population since 2005. She has patrons who range in age from birth to adult, but the teenagers are her favorites. Her library programs have taken her to the county jail, alternative schools, senior centers, day care centers, homeless shelters, public schools, and any area that needs library services. The youthful offenders of the county jail are some of her best patrons. She has published articles about her work with the at-risk population in *Computers and Libraries* and *Young Adult Library Services*. She presented at ALA's annual conference in 2010 and 2012 regarding library services to underserved populations, such as homeless patrons and youth at risk. She will serve on YALSA's Alex Awards Committee for 2013–2015. She received her bachelor's degree in Recreation Administration from Texas State University in 2002 and her master's degree in Library and Information Science in 2009 from the University of South Carolina. She has had many jobs within the public library, starting with circulation services, later joining the outreach department, and then becoming a Children's Manager. Currently she is in the dual role of Teen Services Coordinator and Teen Loft Manager for the Charlotte Mecklenburg Library of Charlotte, North Carolina. For consultations, workshops, library visits, or online workshop sessions, you may reach her at angelakaycraig@gmail.com.

Chantell L. McDowell grew up in the East New York section of Brooklyn, New York, as an at-risk teen. Her desire to give back to her community and help at-risk teens was cultivated as she began her career as a librarian for the Brooklyn Public Library in 2008. She facilitated outreach to public and alternative schools, the Spofford Juvenile Detention Center, Rikers Island, group homes, and neighborhood clinics. The youth who resided in the "Brooklyn Projects" inspired her to help those who struggle. Working with teenagers, especially those at risk, is her passion, because she knows what it feels like to be considered "at risk." While serving as a Teen Services Librarian for the Charlotte Mecklenburg Library of Charlotte, North Carolina, she helped redesign the teen space of the North County Regional Library and provided special programs and services for teens at her library branch. Chantell is currently the Head Library Media Specialist at Ranson International Baccalaureate Middle School in Charlotte, where she is working with an at-risk population and developing several effective library programs that will improve the behavior and learning patterns for an entire community of scholars. Chantell received her bachelor's degree from SUNY Old Westbury, New York, and her master's degree in Information and Library Sciences from Pratt Institute, Brooklyn. She is currently a candidate for her doctoratal degree in Organizational Leadership at Franklin Pierce University, New Hampshire, with plans to develop, implement, and research an effective program that would increase adolescent development and reduce incidents of delinquency, substance use, and academic failure in our disadvantaged youth. She presented at ALA's annual conference in 2012 regarding library services to underserved populations. For consultations, workshops, library visits, or online workshop sessions, you may reach her at chantellmcdowell1@gmail.com.